Pioneer Life
or
Thirty Years a Hunter

PHILIP TOME

Foreword by Robert Wegner

Preface by Henry W. Shoemaker
Appendix by A. Monroe Aurand Jr.

STACKPOLE
BOOKS

0 11557 03324 3

New foreword copyright © 2006 by Robert Wegner

Published by
STACKPOLE BOOKS
5067 Ritter Road
Mechanicsburg, PA 17055
www.stackpolebooks.com

Printed in the United States

10 9 8 7 6 5 4 3 2 1

Cover design by Caroline M. Stover

Library of Congress Cataloging-in-Publication Data

Tome, Philip, 1782–1855.
  Pioneer life, or Thirty years a hunter / Philip Tome ; foreword by Robert Wegner.
    p. cm. — (Classics of American sport)
  Originally published: Harrisburg, Pa. : Aurand press, 1928.
  ISBN-13: 978-0-8117-3324-3 (alk. paper)
  ISBN-10: 0-8117-3324-6 (alk. paper)
    1. Frontier and pioneer life—Pennsylvania. 2. Hunting—Pennsylvania—History—19th century. 3. Pennsylvania—Description and travel. 4. Tome, Philip, 1782–1855.
I. Title. II. Title: Thirty years a hunter. III. Title: Pioneer life. IV. Series.
F153.T65 2006
974.8'03—dc22
                                                                  2006044251

FOREWORD

*With the true hunter it is not the destruction of life which
affords the pleasure of the chase; it is the excitement attendant
upon the very uncertainty of it which induces men even to
leave luxurious homes and expose themselves to the hardships
and perils of the wilderness.*

—Philip Tome, 1854

Throughout the pioneer stage of American history, frontier farmers
depended as much upon venison for their existence as their cultivated
crops and livestock. Every pioneer farmer was a deer hunter; they all had
to be. The whitetail supplied them with deerskins and venison, which they
used to barter for much-needed supplies. But some of these pioneers so
enjoyed the deer hunt they said farewell to the plough to hunt full time.

Perhaps the most famous of these backwoods hunters was Philip
Tome (1782–1855), the Pine Creek deerslayer of the Alleghenies, who
wrote the classic *Pioneer Life, or Thirty Years a Hunter* (1854). "This
indomitable, Indian-looking Nimrod," as Pennsylvania historian Henry
W. Shoemaker called him, had one ambition: to challenge the wiles of the
whitetail in such a way that every hazard favored his adversary. In his
Extinct Pennsylvania Animals (1917), Col. Shoemaker called Tome, "the
greatest of all Pennsylvania hunters of big game. He was a sportsman as
well as a hunter, never killing recklessly."

Like his predecessors, this pioneer farmer-turned-deerslayer viewed
white-tailed deer hunts as arduous military campaigns in which he had to
blaze trails through dense, virgin underbrush ten to twelve miles at a time,
taking only short catnaps in hollow trees or in the skins of freshly killed
black bears. These Homeric deer hunts in the Grand Canyon of the

Alleghenies lasted months at a time, frequently ending when the snow melted and the deer tracks disappeared. He traveled the mountainous terrain of the Alleghenies by canoe, horse, and sleigh, frequently hiring porters, cooks and camp-keepers to assist him in the everyday activities of pioneer life.

From his earliest boyhood in the Pine Creek Valley of Pennsylvania's Lycoming County, Philip Tome was familiar with the rugged life of the frontiersman. At the age of twelve, he shot deer with his father, Jacob Tome (1758–1814), firing an old Jaeger flintlock smooth-bore musket loaded with buckshot, and he mastered the language of the Seneca Indians.

He quickly learned the secrets of hunting deer. He rattled antlers to attract bucks, snorted to stop them in their tracks, and grunted to lure them into the vicinity of his shooting platforms. He built fences around cornfields to entice and entrap does, which he then used as decoys for killing bucks during the rut. Like his Indian comrades, he loved living in quickly-improvised hemlock shanties, cooking trout and venison steaks over a campfire. He was especially proud of the trophy skull he nailed to the top of his hemlock lean-to.

Like most deer hunters, Tome served an apprenticeship with his father, but he also learned his early hunting lessons from an old Pennsylvania buck hunter named John Mills, a pioneer farmer who was so taken with deer hunting that he eventually quit farming and left to hunt the Canadian wilderness. Before going, he offered to sell Tome one of his cherished deer hounds and teach the young lad all he knew about white-tailed deer and deer hunting for the sum of fifteen dollars; Tome accepted.

By the second decade of the nineteenth century, Tome had established his deer hunting grounds near the headwaters of the Kettle, Pine, Sinnemahoning, and Allegheny Rivers. In this area, especially the section near Pine Creek and Stump Creek, he killed a large number of white-tailed deer with his new .45 caliber Kentucky-style flintlock rifle made by E. Remington II (known as "Lite" around 1818). Tome dubbed the rifle "Sure Kill." He used some of the meat for his own purposes, but most of it he salted, cured, and rafted downstream to be sold in the settlements along the river.

Tome was a good-natured man, rugged, muscular, active, and not easily frightened by anything. One pioneer settler, J. M. English of Jersey Shore, Pennsylvania, observed Tome pick up a barrel of whiskey and take a drink out of the bung hole at Irving Stephenson's Tavern at the mouth of Pine Creek. As Tome himself admitted, he "was never conquered by any man or animal."

By the age of eighteen, Tome was clearly comfortable in the company of wolves and whitetails. While hunting deer in October of 1800 along the banks of Pine Creek in Lycoming County, he was surrounded by wolves. "Their unearthly howling," Tome recalls in his autobiography, "mingled with the dismal screeching of the owls overhead made a concert of sounds that banished sleep from my eyes the greater part of the night. I sat in my shanty, with my gun in one hand, a tomahawk in the other, and a knife by my side. When the wolves became unusually uproarious, I would send the dog out to drive them away, and if they drove him back in, I would fire in among them. At length, toward morning, I fell asleep from sheer exhaustion and slept until daylight, when I arose, ate my breakfast and started again on the deer track."

While hunting and tracking deer, Tome used the wolves to his advantage. "We could hear the wolves and foxes howling and barking in our rear, guided by our fires," Tome records. "We encouraged them in pursuing the deer. . . . The wolves and our dogs hunted together, sometimes one and sometimes the other obtained the deer and if it fell into our hands we always left the wolves their portion to keep them near, for we considered them of great assistance to us in deer hunting."

Tome employed various methods of hunting: fire hunting, stalking, hounding, and stand hunting in elevated platforms over salt licks. He favored fire hunting from the first of June to mid-January. Although fire hunting deer was banned in Mississippi and Alabama as early as 1803, and prohibited in Florida in 1828, it wasn't banned in various counties in Pennsylvania until 1848. In his autobiography he describes this way of deer hunting:

"The deer would come to the river after dark to eat the moss which grew on the bottom and collect together about the ripples in groups of from three to ten. The hunters would build a fire of yellow pitch pine in the middle of a canoe and station a man in the stern to steer and one or two more in front to fire at the deer. When there were no deer in sight they could push and paddle the canoe along. When they came within sight of the deer the canoe was allowed to float down with the current, and the steersman laid it in a position the most advantageous for those who were in the bow with guns. The deer would generally raise their heads and stand looking at the fire until the canoe came within a few yards of them.

"The hunters could judge by their movements whether they would make a break or stand still until they came near them, and fired or not according to the movements of the deer. When the deer attempted to run out of the water where the bank was bluff and steep, they would see their own shadows and thinking it was a dog or a wolf, would utter a snort and spring back into the water, sometimes coming near enough to the canoe to give the hunter two or three more shots at them."

In this manner Tome sometimes killed four deer in one place. After field dressing the deer, he laid the venison on shore and proceeded down the river in search of another group. Some nights he shot as many as ten whitetails. On his return he would fish for salmon and pick up the venison as he came along. His canoes could carry up to 4,000 pounds safely; when he returned to his log cabin in the morning, he had enough salmon and venison to feed a family for two months. On one occasion while fire hunting deer along the banks of Pine Creek with a Nimrod named Clark from Vermont, Tome got one deer without even firing old "Sure Kill":

"Pushing up the stream about seven miles, we turned and commenced floating down at nine o'clock. After proceeding about a mile, Clark, who sat forward, saw a large buck, a short distance ahead. He fired and wounded the animal, when it wheeled and attempted to plunge over the canoe. Clark held up his hand to protect himself, which frightened the buck still more; he sprang across the canoe giving Clark a blow between the eyes with its hind feet, knocking him prostrate. I asked him if he was hurt, and he replied that he was nearly killed. I pushed ashore as soon as possible, and took him out of the canoe. His face was bathed in blood and presented a ghastly appearance. Upon washing away the blood I discovered that he was not as badly injured as I had feared. There was a severe contusion in the spot where he was struck, but the skin was not broken; the blood had dropped from the wounded deer.

"I then went after the deer which I found lying down badly wounded but not dead. I finished it with a ball through the head and dragged it to the canoe. We floated down a mile, when we saw a buck and doe eating moss. Clark fired, killing the buck and the doe ran ashore, when, becoming frightened at her shadow, she leaped back toward the canoe. As she raised to spring over, I hit her on the nose with a paddle, and she fell back into the canoe, when I cut her throat. We then floated down, picked up our buck, and proceeded homeward with three deer, one of which had not cost us even a shot."

On another occasion, it seemed that even an infinite supply of gunpowder and lead from "Sure Kill" could not down the deer.

"About the middle of July in 1805, Morrison, Francis and myself were out on a hunt. Going up the creek about five miles, we commenced floating down, and soon shot a deer, which we stowed away in our canoe. When we had gone a short distance farther, two of us saw a deer in the stream and both fired at the same time but neither appeared to hit it. We re-loaded and directed the man who was steering to run the canoe to the shore. We then stood on the shore, about thirty rods from the deer and each fired eight shots at it, as rapidly as we could load, when our guns became so hot that we were compelled to stop. The steersman had been holding up the torch for us to see by, yet the position of the animal was the same as when first observed. At each shot it seemed to spring up, each time higher and higher, then dropping into the same spot. We then threw sticks at it, to drive it away, when it gave two or three leaps and suddenly disappeared. This affair may appear somewhat strange to the reader, as it did to me, but the facts are as I have stated, and always appeared to me unaccountable."

Expecting his deer hunting campaigns to last about six weeks at a time, Tome always took along an abundant supply of provisions. For four hunters he packed flour, potatoes, sugar, chocolate, corn, and a good quantity of salt to cure the venison. Additionally, they brought six empty barrels for the meat, an iron pot holding about six gallons, a camp kettle, four axes, a broadax, a chalk line, a canoe howel (an instrument for scooping water out of canoes), a drawing knife, two augers, six tomahawks, and three to four pounds of gunpowder and lead. Each hunter took a rifle and a musket, two knives, a quart cup, four shirts, two blankets, and a good supply of soap. Thus equipped and accompanied by four deer hounds, Tome and his comrades pushed upstream with their hewed-out canoe; two hunters in the canoe and the other two hunting along the shore.

The augers Tome carried with him he used to bore holes in black oak logs into which he poured three pints of salt and a small quantity of saltpeter. He would then insert a plug in each hole. He found that when the wood became saturated with salt, the deer would gnaw at it. When the deer responded to his salt lick, he immediately built a scaffold within three to four rods of the salt so that the deer would become accustomed to the sight of it. Tome traveled from deer lick to deer lick—from Stony Lick to Mud Lick to Rock Lick—for all these deer licks were eventually named and placed on the hunting maps of his time. His travels frequently ended at Irving Stephenson's Tavern at the mouth of Pine Creek, where in the company of other deerslayers and pioneer farmers he ate venison jerky, drank wine freely, talked about deer, and expanded upon the deer hunting stories of the time.

Tome also enjoyed hunting deer with hounds, a practice legal in Pennsylvania until 1897. He kept two large deer hounds for this purpose and believed that the best dog for deer hunting was a "half bloodhound, a quarter cur and the other quarter greyhound." Proud of his hounds, Tome boasted in *Pioneer Life* that "when they were once in chase of a deer, they would not lose one in ten. So famous did they become for their prowess, that if any of the neighbors saw them running, they would exclaim, 'There are Tome's dogs; the deer cannot be far off.' The deer could never baffle them by any of their usual stratagems, and they would often run them down before they reached the water. Those wishing to deer hunt successfully should always procure, at any cost, the largest and best dogs to be found."

Between deer hunts, Tome conducted a profitable business of capturing elk alive, exhibiting them to interested spectators, and then selling them alive for as much as $500 a head. With the aid of his dog and a Native American named Billy Fox, Tome captured several live, full-grown elk along the banks of the Susquehanna. In 1816, according to McKnight's *History of Northwestern Pennsylvania*, Tome caught the largest elk ever secured in Pennsylvania. Using ropes, poles, nooses, horses, and four hunting hounds, and after giving chase for fourteen strenuous miles, Tome and his party finally brought an elk that "stood sixteen hands high and had antlers six feet long with eleven points on each side" to bay on a large rock and promptly anchored the animal to surrounding trees. Tome successfully managed to get the elk alive to the Allegheny River in sub-zero weather. He then floated the animal on a raft to Olean Point and from there traveled with the elk through New York State to Albany, exhibiting him for profit. At Albany, Tome sold the elk for $500.

In his deer hunting memoirs, Tome reports that in one deer season that lasted from June until mid-January he killed 137 white-tailed deer, and during his lifetime he killed more than 1,000 deer. He usually averaged 130 big-game animals per season. His descendants estimate that at least 500 noble panthers fell to Tome's bullets. Tome maintained a strong ethical code and wrote these words at the age of seventy-two:

"I never wantonly killed a deer, when I could gain nothing by its destruction. With the true hunter it is not the destruction of life which affords the pleasure of the chase; it is the excitement attendant upon the very uncertainty of it which induces men even to leave luxurious homes and expose themselves to the hardships and perils of the wilderness. Even when, after a weary chase, the game is brought down, he cannot, after the first thrill of triumph, look without a pang of remorse, upon the form which was so beautifully adapted to its situation, and which his hand has reduced to a mere lump of flesh."

For more than sixty years, Tome roamed the Pine Creek Valley west to the Allegheny River, east to the west branch of the Susquehanna, south to the Clarion River, and north into New York to hunt deer along the banks of the Susquehanna. He often traveled twenty to thirty miles a day, frequently confronting 450-pound black bear in their dens. He killed bears while they slept and then slept himself in bear and panther dens, when he didn't have time to construct a shanty of hemlock brush.

In December of 1818, he started out on a deer hunting expedition with John Campbell, a Warren County deerslayer; Joseph Darling, a sawmill owner; and his Seneca deer-hunting partner, Billy Fox. Before the year ended, according to Pennsylvania folklore, this adventurous foursome traveled to Buckville, New York, and participated in one of the most famous deer drives in the history of this country. In *Early Times on the Susquehanna* (1870), historian Mrs. George A. Perkins chronicles this deer drive—200 men armed with hounds, horses, guns, and rifles. Some came from Pennsylvania and others from New York, and all came with great gusto:

> "Up men! arouse for the chase!
> The wild buck is quitting his lair,
> The hills are gilded with light,
> And there's health in the balmy air."

The drivers formed a circle of men several miles in extent with the "marshals of the day, at the head of their respective commands, and clothed with due authority." The line of the New York drivers stretched from Chemung River, near Buckville, across the hills to Shepard's Creek on the north. As they approached their rendezvous, the woods rang out with rifle shots. In the heat of the excitement, the anxious men shot in every direction and, as Mrs. Perkins notes, "with rashness and reckless-ness." Many a buck fell as did one die-hard, Pennsylvania deerslayer him-self named Big Decker. But his wound was only slight, and Big Decker finished the ordeal in the upright position still riding his horse into battle.

When the belching smoke pipes fell silent, the deerslayers dressed, skinned, and divided thirty white-tailed deer. As the hunters dispersed to their respective settlements, Tome, Campbell, and Billy Fox departed for the Grand Canyon of Pine Creek Valley, their hewed-out canoes filled with deerskins and venison.

Philip Tome was no crude, backwoods barbarian. In his *Pioneer Life*, we learn that he read extensively and enjoyed a good command of the English language. Historians suspect that in addition to reading the novels of James Fenimore Cooper, he also read Sir Walter Scott and Henry W. Longfellow.

He was a keen student of deer behavior. Because of his interest in the animal, he probably read the standard work on the subject: Dr. John Godman's classic essay "The Common Deer," published in his popular *American Natural History* (1826) went through many editions during Tome's lifetime. He also read the leading sportsmen's journals of the day: *Spirit of the Times* and *American Turf Register and Sporting Magazine*.

As an interpreter for Cornplanter and Governor Blacksnake, Indian chiefs of the Allegheny River, Tome was respected by the Seneca Indians, who admired his character, integrity, and honesty. Tome was also acquainted with Red Jacket and Black Hawk. When Tome was eighteen in 1790, he recorded verbatim Cornplanter's famous speech to President Washington in Philadelphia. Tome's hunting companions were well-to-do gentlemen, businessmen, and others who emerged as leaders in colonial Pennsylvania.

Historians recognize Tome as more than an ordinary deer hunter. Charles Sheldon, collector and curator of a fine library of North American big-game hunting books, classifies Tome's *Pioneer Life* as "remarkable and accurate and one of the prize books of my library."

Henry W. Shoemaker, prominent chronicler of America's deer-hunting legends, tales, and folklore and pioneer chairman of the Pennsylvania Historical Commission, recommended *Pioneer Life* "as the great and outstanding contemporary narrative of the Pennsylvania big game fields . . . and one of the most valuable and interesting records of early frontier life and history relative to the State of Pennsylvania."

To promote Pennsylvania's heritage, Shoemaker edited and published a new edition of Tome's autobiography in 1928, and the *Saturday Review of Literature* reviewed it as "a source book for the mores of the fringe of the first American frontier." Today the edition remains one of the rarest works on the American pioneer hunter and the best example of early nineteenth-century life in Pennsylvania's deer woods. This 1928 edition, limited to 500 signed copies, if found today in the out-of-print book market, sells for approximately $500. According to an unpublished letter written by Tome's wife, Mary, and dated October 22, 1855, the book sold for 72 cents in 1855.

I have collected blue-chip deer books for more than thirty-five years and have seen only one original copy listed in an out-of-print book catalog. Callahan & Company Booksellers' Catalogue #86 published in May 1996 listed the 1854 Buffalo imprint in original binding for $4,500. In 1971, Arno Press and *The New York Times* reprinted the original 1854 edition as part of their First American Frontier series from a rare copy owned by the Wisconsin State Historical Society. Unfortunately, that inexpensive edition is out of print. *Books in Print* (2003) lists the 1991 edition, published by the Reprint Services Corporation, as still in print for $69.

Philip Tome died on April 30, 1855, in Corydon on the Allegheny at the age of seventy-three. He is buried near Chief Cornplanter in the Riverview-Corydon Cemetery on a hill above the Allegheny Reservoir just below the New York State line. In 1989, several Tome descendants erected a new marker engraved with two white-tailed deer—a buck and a doe eating vegetation along the banks of the Allegheny.

In 1855, the year of Tome's death, A. F. Tait issued his famous deer print "Still Hunting on the First Snow: A Second Shot," later reprinted by Currier and Ives as "Deer Shooting on the Shattagee." In 1855, Henry W. Longfellow (1807–1882), published *The Song of Hiawatha*. These works portray the deerslayer as cultural hero. Hiawatha hunts red deer with a bow made from a branch of ash and arrows from an oak bough. Clad in deerskin shirt and buckskin leggings, Hiawatha encounters a roebuck. Had Tome lived longer, he might have recited from memory the following lines:

> Then, upon one knee uprising,
> Hiawatha aimed an arrow;
> Scarce a twig moved with his motion,
> Scarce a leaf was stirred or rustled,
> But the wary roebuck started,
> Stamped with all his hoofs together,
> Listened with one foot uplifted,
> Leaped as if to meet the arrow;
> Ah! the stinging, fatal arrow,
> Like a wasp it buzzed and stung him!
> Dead he lay there in the forest.

By the ford across the river;
Beat his timid heart no longer,
But the heart of Hiawatha
Throbbed and shouted and exulted,
As he bore the red deer homeward.

Although the early American deerslayers killed thousands of deer by the end of the nineteenth century, as the whitetail became more scarce hunters gave up market hunting. Though nostalgic for the wilder hunting days of the past, they began to champion a code of sporting ethics. While they did not regret the commercial hunting of the past, they proposed a wiser use of the natural resource.

In their writings, they emphasized combining the study of nature with the hunting experience and called for restraint in hunting methods and appetites.

Changing his attitude later in life, Philip Tome deemphasized the importance of the kill, or the number of kills, and underscored instead the tonic quality of the outdoor experience and the redemptive and educational aspects of the deer-hunting ceremony and ritual. Deer hunting must become an art, he insisted, an ennobling and instructive ceremony in which the hunter confirms his manhood in the deer forest but not at the expense of the natural resource.

By the second half of the nineteenth century, the hunter-naturalist was emerging in America. While Tome did not see the development of this movement, he had abandoned his market gunning in favor of a firm commitment to conservation and a code of sportsmanship. Had he lived longer, I think he would have wandered the deer forest for science and sport like his hunter-naturalist descendants.

Reliving the adventures of Philip Tome, we pay tribute to America's deer-hunting heritage and help ensure its future for the twelve million deer hunters in America who pursue the thirty-two million white-tailed deer with the same enthusiasm and determination of the Pine Creek deerslayer.

Robert Wegner
Deer Valley
Summer 2005

REFERENCES

Beck, Harold Thomas. "Cornplanter's Wager." *The Mountain Laurel Review*. 1998. www.mlrmag.com.

Bronner, Simon J. *Popularizing Pennsylvania: Henry W. Shoemaker and the Progressive Uses of Folklore and History*. Pennsylvania: Pennsylvania State University Press, 1996.

Cooper, James Fenimore. *The Deerslayer*. Philadelphia: Lea & Blanchard, 1841.

Forbes, Stanlely E. , et. al. *The White-Tailed Deer in Pennsylvania*. Pennsylvania: The Pennsylvania Game Commission, 1971.

Frederick, Paul. "Philip Tome: Legendary Hunter." www.allegheny-online.com.

Kosack, Joe. *The Pennsylvania Game Commission, 1895–1995: 100 Years of Wildlife Conservation*. Pennsylvania: The Pennsylvania Game Commission, 1995.

Kraybill, Spencer L. *Pennsylvania's Pine Creek Valley*. Maryland: Gateway Press, 1991.

Longfellow, Henry W. *The Song of Hiawatha*. Boston: Ticknor and Fields, 1855.

Neal, Don. "The Allegheny Elk Hunter." *Pennsylvania Game News*. February 1959. pp. 22–27.

Pennsylvania Atlas & Gazetteer. Maine: DeLorme, 2001.

Perkins, Mr. George A. "The Deer Hunt of 1818." *Early Times on the Susquehanna*. Pennsylvania: The Herald Company of Binghamton, 1870. pp. 181–185.

Rinkus, Gregg. "Wilderness Adventures of Philip Tome." *Pennsylvania Game News*. 77(4): 18–22. April 2006.

Russell, Helen H. "Philip Tome, 1782–1885, Was Pioneer, Hunter, Author, Man of Many Skills." *The Express*. Lock Haven, Pennsylvania, Saturday, February 6, 1965. pp. 13–14.

———. "Philip Tome Had Indians' Trust as Their Agent and Interpreter." *The Express*. Lock Haven, Pennsylvania, Saturday, February 16, 1965. pp. 15–17.

Sajna, Mike. *Buck Fever: The Deer Hunting Tradition in Pennsylvania*. Pennsylvania: Univeristy of Pittsburgh Press, 1990.

Shoemaker, Henry W. *Pennsylvania Deer and Their Horns*. Pennsylvania: The Faust Printing Company, 1915.

Tome, Philip. *Pioneer Life; or, Thirty Years a Hunter*. Buffalo, 1854. (First edition.)

———. *Pioneer Life; or, Thirty Years a Hunter*. Harrisburg, Pennsylvania: Aurand Press, 1928.

———. *Pioneer Life; or, Thirty Years a Hunter*. New York: Arno Press, 1971.

———. *Pioneer Life; or, Thirty Years a Hunter*. Massachusetts: Ayer, 1989.

———. *Pioneer Life; or, Thirty Years a Hunter*. Baltimore: Gateway Press, 1991. (Reprint of the 1928 edition with an index by the Lycoming County Genealogical Society.)

Van Dyne, Ed. "The Mighty Nimrod of Pine Creek." *Pennsylvania Game News*. 32(7): 22–25. July 1961.

Wegner, Robert. *Wegner's Bibliography on Deer & Deer Hunting*. Wisconsn: St. Hubert's Press, 1992.

———. *Legendary Deer Camps*. Wisconsin: Krause Publications, 2001.

———. "A Pioneer Deerslayer." *Deer & Deer Hunting*. 10(5): 8–14. June 1987.

PREFACE TO THE PRESENT EDITION.

WITH the republication of *Pioneer Life; or, Thirty Years a Hunter,* by Philip Tome, with notes and an Appendix, the undersigned feels that it has fallen to his lot, with Mr. A. M. Aurand, Jr., to help preserve one of the most valuable and interesting records of early frontier life and history relative to the State of Pennsylvania.

But few copies of the small edition published by the Author in 1854, are known to exist, and the last four copies sold at retail, second-hand, at an average of $125.00 a copy. Evidently it must be scarce — neither the Library of Congress, Pennsylvania State Library, New York Public Library, nor any of the other large historical libraries are known to have a copy, save one, a library in Wisconsin. A copy was presented to the Public Library, Williamsport. One copy is in Baltimore, privately owned; three in Warren county, Pa., (two of them being in one library), and two copies in the library of the undersigned. Of these few, the last known copy to come on the book auction market, was sold at the Anderson Galleries, New York, March, 1928, for $140.00, going to a man in Chicago.

The narrative is important in its relation to Pennsylvania history — north and west. As the book has been in constant demand for years, the difficulty of ever reprinting it became more apparent, with the passing of the years, and no copies turning up on the second-hand book market. The larger libraries being without a copy, could not loan it. However, the public are indebted to a scholarly gentleman who loaned a copy to Mr. Aurand, Jr., the present publisher, and from which the story, as it appears again, has been reprinted word for word.

The reader will find some Annotations by the publisher, included in an Appendix, which have been sifted from various reliable sources. It is inconceivable that doubts have been cast on the authenticity of Philip Tome as a hunter, chronicler, and even as an individual. In the vicinity of Corydon, Warren county, where he spent his last days he is well remembered, and the handsome home occupied by his grandson, George L. Tome, testifies to the prominence of the family in that locality. George Tome's daughter, Mrs. John Reid, occupies an enviable position in literary and social circles at Oil City, where she is President of the Belles Lettres Club.

While Philip Tome infers that his ancestry was of German origin, the family were in reality Huguenots, Gascons in fact, where, in the vicinity of Auch, several variants of the name are found. The present spelling of the name "TOME" is nearer to the original French forms than the later German ones. As the result of religious persecutions they escaped to Switzerland, and later to the Palatinate, from whence they migrated to Pennsylvania.

The intermarriage of members of the Tome family with the Gamble, Humes, and Blackwell families who were among the leading families of the Upper West Branch Valley of Pennsylvania in Revolutionary days, shows that the Tomes were affiliated with the best types of people of that region in the earliest times, and accounts for the uncommonly good English that Philip Tome wrote. The late Theodore Roosevelt once said that no matter how thrilling a hunting narrative might be it had no appeal to him if it was not good literature. To such an exacting standard *Pioneer Life, or Thirty Years a Hunter* would meet the erudite "faunal naturalist's" views exactly. As a work of literature, as well as of absorbing interest this book by Philip Tome can be unhesitatingly recommended as the great, outstanding contemporary narrative of the Pennsylvania big game fields.

HENRY W. SHOEMAKER,
Chairman of the Pennsylvania Historical Commission,
STATE LIBRARY, HARRISBURG, PA.
August 15, 1928.

INTRODUCTION.

IN presenting the following incidents of my life, to the public, I do not intend to claim for it beauty of expression, for it is the production of one born in the wilderness; one who is more conversant with the howl of the wolf and panther, and the whoop of the savage, than the tones of oratory, as heard in civilized life.

It is said that truth is often more strange than fiction; and those in pursuit of the marvelous will not be disappointed in perusing these pages, as they are full of scenes in Border Life, accidents, and hair-breadth escapes.

The lover of the hunt will find faithfully portrayed, the exciting scenes of the chase, the fight with the elk, the wolf and the panther, and herein be enabled to gather the experience of nearly half a century as to the best mode of securing every description of game to be found in our forests.

The general reader will find it replete with scenes of wild, stirring and thrilling interest; it being the narrative of one who, in all the scenes of border life was never conquered by man or animal.   P. T.

CORYDON, PA., *April,* 1854.

CONTENTS.

Pioneer Life

CHAPTER I.

BIRTH AND EARLY LIFE.

I WAS born March 22d, 1782, in Dauphin County, Pennsylvania, near where the city of Harrisburg now stands. My parents were both of German extraction. They moved up the Susquehannah River about ninety miles in 1786, traveling in a keel boat, there being no roads or other mode of conveyance. They landed at a place called Farris creek in what was then Northumberland county, and remained there about four months, when the Six Nations of Indians began to trouble the inhabitants on the west branch of the Susquehannah. We then moved back into Cumberland county, five miles from Harrisburg, on the west side of the Susquehannah. At that time the Indians distressed the inhabitants for about eighteen months. We remained there two or three years, when, the Indians having become peaceable, we returned up the river, and stopped at Warry Run, about two miles above the junction of the two branches of the Susquehannah.

In 1791, my father purchased some land about seventy miles up the west branch of the river in the wilderness. He hired men and paid them in advance to build a house. They did not fulfil their contract, but having raised and enclosed it, left it without chimney, door, window, or floor, while the bushes ten feet high were left standing in the middle of the house. On the first of November my father started for his residence, and loaded a keel boat with provisions sufficient for one year, irons for a mill, and a supply of clothing. He was six days going fifty miles. He then arrived at the mouth of Pine Creek, six miles from his destination, but could proceed no farther with his boat, on account of low water. He then hired ten canoes, and started with such articles as he most needed. He arrived at his house the 20th of November.

It was very cold; the men had been dragging the boats, and the women were nearly frozen. When within two miles of the house two of the men who assisted in building it asked the privilege of going ahead to make a fire. When we arrived in sight we saw a large fire, which revived our spirits greatly, for the snow was falling rapidly, the wind blew cold, and we were chilled through. A hole had been left for a chimney, and a fire built on that side of the house, and when we arrived the men were cutting out the brush. My father asked why things had been left in this state. They replied that they could not induce the other men to proceed any farther with the job. Father then demanded why they had not informed him a day or two earlier, and was inclined to be somewhat angry, when my mother interposed, and said if we could get through the first night it would do. We soon became warm, had our supper, went to sleep and passed the night very comfortably. The next morning all hands went to work and made a floor and chimney, and plastered the house, and accomplished it in two days. On the 25th my father commenced his mill. He had to hew and split out all the timbers to be used for building. He had also a race to dig and a dam to build, and he had it all finished by the first of March.

At that time game, such as bears, elk, deer and wild turkeys were very plenty in that section of the country. I had two brothers old enough to hunt, but they had no gun except an old musket which my father had used while training. In the morning we would frequently find the deer feeding within twenty rods of the house. Sometimes we would see a drove of elk, fifteen or twenty in number, crossing the river. At other times we saw bears traveling back and forward. But we had no hunters among the six men, and no gun but the old musket, and that was out of order. On the 5th of December two of our nearest neighbors, (who lived twelve miles distant) came to see us, bringing two guns and two dogs, but no ammunition. There was no powder or lead in that part of the country except what my father had, and he supplied them what they needed. They then hunted about two days for my father to procure him a supply of wild meat. Notwithstanding they were little skilled in hunting, and the weather was unfavorable, they killed four deer, and two large fat bears.

The nearest grist-mill was thirty miles distant, and no road or other means of getting to it; nor had we any grain except a little which we raised in the same manner as the Indians. Every family had what was called a " family block " or mortar, in which they pounded their corn into meal and samp.

The inconveniences which people experienced in traveling at that time were great. From the mouth of Pine Creek to the first fork was called twelve miles. The flats extended four miles up the river from the mouth. On the west side a high mountain, with steep, rocky sides hanging over the river rose to the height of two miles and a half. There we had to cross the river, as the mountain was impassable on the northwest side. After traveling a mile on the southeast side, another mountain obstructed our path and turned us back on the west side again. We then traveled about three-fourths of a mile, when we were compelled to recross to the east side, and after continuing about a mile farther, a steep, rocky mountain again intercepted our path, and it became necessary to return to the west side, when we had a flat of nearly two miles on the bank of the river. We then crossed over to the east side and traveled a flat three-fourths of a mile long, thence we crossed to an island which lay in the center of the river. We crossed back to the east side from the island at the mouth of the first fork of Pine Creek.

I will now lay before the reader the height of the mountains, the kind of game that is to be found on them, and other particulars of the country, from the mouth of Pine Creek to the first point. Every family owned a canoe for the purpose of traveling up and down the river. In winter they had good ice to travel on, which lasted about three months. That was the season in which the greatest amount of business was done by the settlers. The mountains were about a mile in height, and abundance of deer, bears, foxes, wolves and panthers, but no elk were found on them.

The most successful mode of killing deer from the first of June to the last of September was to fire-hunt them, which was done in the following manner: The deer would come to the river after dark to eat the moss which grew on the bottom, and collect together about the ripples, in groups from three to ten. The hunters would build a fire of yellow pitch pine in the middle of a canoe and station a man in the

stern to steer, and one or two more in front to fire at the
deer. When there were no deer in sight they could push
and paddle the canoe along. When they came within sight
of the deer the canoe was allowed to float down with the
current, and the steersman laid it in a position the most advantageous for those who were in the bow with guns. The
deer would generally raise their heads and stand looking at
the fire until the canoe came within a few yards of them.
The hunters could judge by their movements whether they
would make a break or stand still until they came near them,
and fired or not according to the movements of the deer.
When the deer attempted to run out of the water where
the bank was bluff and steep, they would see their own shadows, and thinking it was a dog or a wolf, would utter a cry
and spring back into the water, sometimes coming near
enough to the canoe to give the hunters two or three more
shots at them. In this manner they would kill from one
to four deer in one place. Having dressed and laid out the
meat on the shore, they would proceed down the river in
search of another group. If the night was favorable, from
three to ten deer were killed in this manner. On their return they would fish for eels, salmon and other fish, and take
in their venison as they came along. Their canoes were
capable of carrying from 2,000 to 4,000 pounds with safety.
With a five-tined spear they would take from twenty to
sixty eels and a large quantity of salmon; and in the morning return home with fish and venison sufficient to supply
an ordinary family two months.

A woman belonging to a family residing on the bank of
the creek, about half a mile above the first fork, was washing at the creek, accompanied by four or five small children,
when one of them looking up the stream exclaimed, " What
a handsome big red dog is coming! " The animal made a
halt on the top of the bank within fifty feet of the children,
and stood looking at them. Another boy cried " It isn't a
dog; it is a panther! " At that moment a cat came out of
the house, and the panther made a spring at her, when she
ran up a tree, followed by the panther. The cat leaped from
the tree, and the panther seized her just as she struck the
ground. The family hurried into the house and closed the
doors, and thus escaped. After the panther had devoured the
cat he stood looking at the house and moved along the path.
In about half an hour a neighbor came along with a dog and
gun. The panther continued to move slowly off, and the

woman came out and acquainted the neighbor with the circumstances. He immediately started in pursuit, and the
panther being driven up a tree by the dog, was brought to
the ground by a well-aimed shot. It was a very large one,
measuring four and a half feet from the tip of the nose to
the tail.

Two miles from that place, up Big Pine Creek, lived a
family consisting of a man and three females. The house
stood on a flat lying between the river and the rocky bluff,
which rose to the height of forty or fifty feet. In the month
of January the man was absent teaching school, and no one
was left at home but the women. On the morning of a
blustering day in the early part of the month, as one of
the women was going to the river for a pail of water she
heard a scream proceeding from the side of the hill, which
sounded like the voice of a woman in distress. She returned
into the house and told the others that she thought there
was [a] woman on the hill in trouble. They all went to
the door to ascertain the source of the cries, when they saw
moving toward them an animal which they took at first for
a dog. When it had approached within fifty yards, they
discovered to their horror that it was a panther. They retreated into the house and closed the doors. Three geese
which belonged to the family were on the ice of the river;
the panther discovered them, and having captured one, he returned with it to his den among the rocks. After he had
been gone some time, they went out together and procured
wood and water enough to supply them until the next day.
The following morning at about the same hour, the panther
returned, uttering the same terrific cries, and carried away
another of the geese. On the third morning he again made
his appearance and took the remaining goose. He had now
become wonted to the vicinity, and the terrified women were
at a loss what they could do. Their nearest neighbors were
distant two miles in one direction, and three in the other,
and any attempt to procure succor from that source would
expose them to an attack from the animal which was prowl-
ing near. In order to prevent the panther from entering
by the chimney, they covered it over with boards taken from
the floor, and kept up a fire all night. The next morning,
when the too familiar cries of their besieger were heard, they
turned out the dog. The panther closed in with him, drove
him against the door, and after a short struggle killed and
carried him off. The morning following, Rice Hamlin, who

lived about three miles distant, and who had been engaged to call on them once a week, to supply them with fire-wood and render any necessary assistance, paid them his customary visit. When he knocked at the door they demanded who it was that desired admittance. Upon learning who was at the door they opened it at once, and informed him of the visits of their unwelcome neighbor. He entered, and they cleared the house of the smoke, which had become almost suffocating. As he stepped to the door to see if the panther was near, Hamlin heard his scream. He immediately started in pursuit, accompanied by his dog. As they came up, the panther jumped upon a rock about twenty-five feet high. Hamlin did not discover him at first, but kept up a search, supposing him to be up a tree. The dog saw the panther, but being unable to follow, kept running around in an uneasy manner. Hamlin at length happened to look up the rocks and his eyes met those of the panther, just as the latter was about to make a spring upon him. Instantly bringing up his gun, he fired with an unerring aim, and the animal came tumbling heavily to the ground at Hamlin's feet. The ball had penetrated its forehead. It was a very large one, weighing about two hundred pounds.

CHAPTER II.

HUNTING THE ELK.

IN August, 1795, my father, Jacob Tome, Jerry Morrison and myself started for an elk hunt. Taking salt and flour with us, we pushed up our canoe to a place called Round Island. After hunting two days among the islands, we became convinced that there were no elk there, although they were sometimes very plenty, collecting at this season in droves Morrison proposed that we should proceed to a point called Stony Lick, about seven miles back, on the east side of the river, at the second fork of Pine Creek, and twelve miles above their junction. My father readily consented to the proposal, as Morrison was an older and more experienced hunter than he. When we arrived within two miles of the Lick, we discovered the tracks of two elks, a buck and a doe. We followed the tracks about half a mile, when we judged by the indications that they had taken a great leap, as if suddenly frightened. The trails from that place took a different direction. My father and Morrison followed the buck, while I took the track of the doe, keeping sight of my companions at the same time. Before I had proceeded far, I found some of the small intestines of the doe upon the ground. I called to the others to come, and before they arrived I found the entrails strewn all along the track. My companions now came up, and Morrison said it was the work of a panther. After following the track a short distance we found the doe lying dead, and bearing marks which fully confirmed Morrison's conjecture. She was completely disembowelled, her throat torn open, and her blood sucked. We skinned her, salted the meat in the skin, and put it away between two logs. We now resumed our route for Stony Lick, and encamped near there that night. About eight o'clock the next morning, while we were preparing to return to the meat we had left the previous day, and see if it had been disturbed by the panther, we heard the roar of an elk. Morrison decided at once that it was the buck which we had been tracking, and started in pursuit, taking with him his dog. If he could not shoot him, he was to let the dog chase him down. My father and I remained at our encampment waiting to hear the discharge of Morrison's gun. After going half a mile he met the elk coming on his back track, and brought him down at a distance of about sixty yards. We cut off his horns, which were upward of six feet in length, having eleven branches — six on one horn, and five on the other. The carcass weighed between five and six hundred pounds. Our next object was to get him down to the water where we could skin him. This was finally accomplished after three hours dragging and rolling. Father and Morrison commenced skinning the buck, and asked me if I was willing to go where we had left the doe, about three-quarters of a mile distant, and see if it had been disturbed. I readily consented, on condition that they would allow me to take a gun and the two dogs. I was but thirteen years old, and they thought I would not venture so far from them. As I was starting away, I overheard Morrison saying to my father, "You will see him coming back soon." My father, however, said if I started he did not think I would return without seeing the doe. I went, and finding everything undisturbed, returned to my companions. They finished skinning and salting the elk about two o'clock, and Morrison proposed to go himself over to Mud Lick, about two miles distant, on the east branch of the second fork, and see if any elk had been there, while my father and I were to watch for them at Stony Lick. We were to meet in the evening where we had skinned the elk. We went down to the Lick and concealed ourselves behind some logs. My father commenced mending his moccasins, and directed me to watch the Lick. I stationed myself in front of some roots, out of my father's sight. A small stream ran below me, in which were some very fine large trout. The stream was very shallow, and it occurred to me that if I could stop the water, I might throw out some of the trout. So I slipped down to the stream, unperceived by my father, went up past him, threw an old log across, and gathered moss and stopped the water. Then I went below, and threw out some thirty fine large trout. My father looked after me, and seeing what I was doing, asked me laughingly if that was the way I watched the Lick. I replied that I wanted some trout for supper. While I was stringing my fish I heard a stone rattle about a hundred yards below me. I turned, and saw a panther looking at me. I sprang up the bank and informed my father what I had seen. Telling me to keep quiet, and make the dog lie down, he stationed himself behind a root having a hole in it, through which he pointed his gun, and waited the panther's approach. When it had come within three rods of us, it paused, with its fore feet upon the bank, and its mouth open, displaying a formidable array of glistening teeth. My father fired, and it fell back dead. The ball had passed through its open mouth, and broken the vertebræ of the neck. We cut it open and left it there. It was larger than any panther I ever saw before or since, and I have seen some thirty: we supposed it to weigh between two and three hundred pounds. When we returned to the camp we found Morrison there before us. We now brought our venison together, and built a scaffold upon which we placed it to dry. It may be well here to describe the manner of preserving elk's meat in the summer. It is first cut in thin slices, and salted down in the skin. We always carried a bag of salt with us for that purpose. Two large poles are laid across crotches about five feet high, and a number of smaller ones are laid across these. After the meat has lain a sufficient length of time in the skin, it is spread upon this scaffold, and a slow fire built under it. The fire is gradually increased and the meat turned until it is dried through. In this state it is called jerk.

Leaving my father to attend to this, Morrison and I started for home to procure horses with which to draw home our meat, going by way of the creek. It was 12 miles to the first fork, and four miles farther to Morrison's residence. I staid with Morrison that night, and the next day went home, seven miles, took two horses and returned to Morrison's that night. When I arrived there, I found a man from Maryland, who wished to go into the woods and hunt elk. He took our horses, and Morrison's brother-in-law took two others, with which they started for the encampment, which they reached that night. The next day they loaded and came to Morrison's, and the following one we went home to my father's residence with his share of the venison and hides.

CHAPTER III.

CAPTURING A LIVE ELK.

IN 1799, my father being at Irving Stephenson's tavern, at
the mouth of Pine Creek, found there a large collection of
men. A horse called the Blue Dun, was kept there. It was
a very large and powerful horse, and it was with difficulty
that three men could take him from the stable. My father
witnessed the operation, and laughed, saying that he could
take the horse from the stable without any assistance. The
others disputed this stoutly, saying that the horse would
kill him if he attempted it; upon which he offered to bet
twenty dollars that he could perform it. His offer was soon
accepted, and as he had not the money by him, he requested
the loan of twenty dollars of an acquaintance who stood
near. The man readily granted his request, and offered to
go halves with him. He felt confident, from his acquaintance with my father, that he would accomplish it. The
money was accordingly staked. Stevenson then remarked
that four were concerned, two on a side; and proposed to
add to the bet four bottles of wine and four dinners. The
opposite party thought there was no risk, and were willing
to bet any thing; so the proposal was accepted. My father
then stipulated that he should be allowed to strike the horse
just as he chose. The opposite party insisted that he should
not strike the horse, at all, and they finally left the matter
to four men, who decided that he might strike the horse in
any manner he chose, provided he did it no material injury.
He then prepared to go into the stable. When they saw
him so willing to perform his undertaking, they offered to
withdraw the bet, fearing that he would be killed at the first
movement. But my father said " No; what I have said, I
will try to do." As he opened the door and went in, they
tried to persuade him to abandon the undertaking, saying
that he would lose his life. He replied cooly, " I have to
die but once." He went up to the horse and spoke coaxingly,

when it looked ill-natured and turned to kick at him. He struck the horse three times in the flank with his open hand, so sharply that it sounded like the crack of a whip. When he spoke to the horse again he stood and trembled. He then went to the horse's head to put on a bridle, when he appeared restive, and attempted to bite him. He spoke to him again, and struck him three times with a stick which he held in his hands so severely that the third blow brought him to his knees. The animal now seemed subdued, and trembled from head to foot. My father then put the bridle upon him, which had not been done by one man alone for a year. He then spoke to the horse, wheeled him around, and led him out of the stable. Seeing another horse he began to plunge, when my father struck him in the flank three times with his open hand, and the second and third blows brought him to his knees. As he dropped to his knees the last time, my father sprang upon his back. The horse went off very quiet and gentle, and he rode it to water, came back, dismounted, and led him around the yard by the bridle in sight of other horses, but yet he remained quiet and docile. He then made him jump three or four times over a horse-trough, four or five feet high. He now told the others that if they would give him a bottle of wine he would take him up a flight of stairs that led to the chamber-floor of the barn. They said if he would do it they would give him five bottles of wine. He took the horse by the bridle, and led him up the stairs and down, when they gave up the bets. The whole party began to drink wine pretty freely and to talk about elk-hunting. Stevenson stepped up to my father and asked him if he could catch a live elk. He replied that he could; when Stevenson offered to bet him on it. My father asked him what he was willing to bet. Stevenson said he was willing to go any length, and would bet two hundred and fifty pounds. My father said he would accept the bet. Stevenson pledged a house, lot and tanyard worth about the amount, and my father gave $750 worth of lumber, and two satisfactory sureties as security for the performance of the undertaking. The elk was to be between fourteen and sixteen hands high, and was to be caught alive and brought home in less than four months. My father finally asked to the middle of February, as there might be no snow in the early part of the winter to enable him to track them. Stevenson said he might have till the first of March if he wished. The articles of agreement were drawn, the security given and the bargain concluded. It was then considered impossible to catch an elk alive, and all the old hunters said it was lost money.

The first of January, 1800, he prepared for his hunt, and started, taking two of his boys and a man named Maddock, with a horse, four dogs, and ropes sufficient to hold an elk. They ascended on the ice eight miles to Morrison's, told him what he had undertaken, and requested him to go with them, as they wished to get his dog, which was good to hunt elk. Morrison declined going, as he considered an attempt to capture an animal so powerful and dangerous to be attended with much peril, and chose to keep out of harm's way. My father therefore concluded to try it the next morning with the help he then had. We accordingly started out on the east side of Pine Creek, up a small stream called Trout Run, which we ascended seven miles. We then came to a spot where the signs in the snow indicated that six or seven elk had been about a week before. We determined to encamp there for the night; and as the weather was very cold and the snow began to fall, we all set to work with an axe and two tomahawks and built a shanty of hemlock boughs. The next morning, as the wind continued to blow very hard, and the snow was falling rapidly, we concluded to remain there until the weather was more favorable. About eleven o'clock the wind ceased, when we started. We traveled until three, but as the snow had filled up all the niches, we could not find the tracks. The weather being clear and cold, my father proposed that two of us should remain and build a shanty, and the other two start out, each on different routes, to look for elk tracks. My father and older brother started out, while Maddock and I remained to build a shanty. The others came back about sundown. We had our shanty completed, my father officiated as cook, and in our snug walls of hemlock boughs we forgot the toils and perils of the chase. My brother reported that he had seen tracks in a muddy place where the elk had been the night before. The next morning we started about sunrise, and proceeded to the place where Jacob had seen the tracks, arriving there about nine o'clock. The elk had taken a southern direction. When we had followed them about nine miles we came to a place where they had been feeding, and the tracks were quite fresh. They had been gone, as we judged, about two hours. We thought it best not to disturb them that day, as it was nearly night. We accordingly made an encampment and stayed there that night. The following morning, the 5th instant, we started about sunrise, and after following the track about three miles and a half, we found where the elk had lain the night before. About a mile farther we discovered two elk, both bucks, and one a little larger than the other. We tied up all the dogs but one, and let him give them chase. The larger one stood and fought the dog, but the other, as soon as he saw us, turned and started off in another direction, and we let another dog go. As the second dog came up, the elk started off, taking a southeast course to Pine Creek, which he crossed. We all started after him and followed as fast as possible for twelve miles, when we met the dogs coming back. It was now four o'clock in the afternoon, and after proceeding two miles farther, encamped for the night taking care to secure the dogs. The next morning, January 6th, we started before sunrise, and after going about a mile, came to a place where the elk had fought the dogs and beat them back. About a mile farther he began to feed, and there lay down and staid all night. We kept on until we came within sight of him and let the two best dogs go. The elk kept a southeast course about eight miles, the dogs pursuing very closely, when he turned and fought them, as we judged, about half an hour. He then struck a northern or northeast course, to cross Big Pine Creek. He then ran some 4 miles farther, when he again turned and fought the dogs. From there he took a north course and ran about eight miles farther, to the Stony Fork on the second fork of Pine Creek. There he stood in the water and fought the dogs. We came to within two miles of that place and encamped for the night. About midnight the dogs came back to the camp. The old elk-dog appeared very uneasy, looking wishfully in the direction from which they had come in, from which we concluded that the elk could not be far off. In the morning we started again, and soon came to the spot where the dogs had held the elk at bay in the water, as we judged, about four hours. After the elk left the water he had gone about two miles and commenced feeding. When we had proceeded a short distance, we found the elk lying down. He sprang up as we approached, and stood looking at us until we were quite near him. We then let loose the two dogs which had not run the day before. They pursued him very closely about six miles and stopped him, until we came up. We then let the other dogs go, thinking he would go to some rock where he could ward off the attack of the dogs. He however took a southern course toward Big Pine Creek, and after running about four miles, got upon a rock on the side of the hill. But here he was so warmly attacked that he could not maintain his position, and so he started on again, ran about four miles farther, and backed up against the root of an upturned tree, where he again stood at bay. We then endeavored, by standing upon the trunk of the upturned tree, to throw a rope over his horns, but did not succeed. He started again, taking a southerly course toward the second fork of Big Pine Creek, and stopped on a large rock. At sundown we stopped within two miles of him, and one of the party went forward a short distance, and discovered where he was by the barking of the dogs. We then concluded to proceed as it was a bright, moonlight evening, and reached the rock about eight o'clock. We built a large fire within a few feet of the rock, and about eleven o'clock we made the dogs come and lie down by the fire. At two o'clock the elk lay down on the rock and began chewing his cud. In the morning at daylight, he arose, stretched himself, and walked around the rock. We cooked our breakfast, and all hands prepared for the contest. At eight o'clock we began to manœuver. We tried at first to throw the rope over his head, but he jumped from the rock, and broke away. We then let all our dogs after him, and fired our guns to encourage them. He ran about half a mile, but the dogs pursued him so closely, and closed in with him so often, that he wheeled about and returned to the rock. We then concluded to divert his attention to the lower side of the rock by keeping the dogs there and throwing sticks and stones, while father slipped unobserved to the upper side, and with a pole about twenty feet long, threw the noose over his horns. All hands then went on the upper side of the hill, and fastened the rope around a tree, and made an ineffectual attempt to draw him from the rock. We next set the dogs on him behind, which drove him to the edge, when we gave a sudden pull and brought him off the rock, which was there about 4 ft. high. He then plunged around, and became so much entangled that he had only ten feet of play. We then placed another long rope upon the other horn and carried it down the hill its whole length, tied it, and then loosed the first one. Two of the party then drove him down the hill as far as the rope would allow him. We continued in this manner to fasten the ropes alternately until we had worked him from tree to tree down the hill. We found this a slow and difficult manner of proceeding, as he was constantly becoming en[t]angled, by his struggles, among the trees and under-brush. So we unloosed both ropes, and placed two men to each rope, and let one dog keep him going. When he went too fast, we could check him by snubbing the rope around a tree. He started and walked very gently till he reached the creek, which was covered with ice. This was about three-fourths of a mile from the rock where he was captured. We fastened one rope across the creek, which was about three rods wide, keeping the other in our hands, and drove him upon the ice, when he slipped and made several ineffectual attempts to regain his feet. We all went to the other side of the creek and dragged him across. As soon as he gained a footing he sprang up and walked up the hill toward us. We then fastened the ropes in opposite directions to give him no play, and as it was now four o'clock in the afternoon, we determined to let him remain here until we could bring a horse from Morrison's, to take him home. We accordingly cut and placed before him some elk-wood browse, which he ate, and my brother and Maddock went for the horse, leaving my father and myself to watch our prize. They returned at eight o'clock the next morning. We had cut a road through the underbrush about one mile to Big Pine Creek. We now secured him close up to a tree, and placed a large rope about forty feet long, over his horns, down near to his head, and then tied a smaller rope to the upper part of each horn. We then attached the horse to the large rope, a man took each a small rope behind; and one of the hands started the horse. When the elk first started, he plunged about con-siderably, and became entangled in the rope; but one of the hands drove him back, and we took a fresh start. At the end of three hours we reached Big Pine Creek, one mile from the place of starting. Here we met with no further obstruc-tion, as the ice was slightly covered with snow and had thawed a little, so that the elk found a good footing. We therefore proceeded without difficulty the next five miles, when we arrived at Morrison's, and placed our captive in a stable. Before we had taken the elk farther a heavy rain came on and broke up the ice in the river. Our horse ran off and was drowned, and we took our elk home, eight miles down the river, on a float. We wrote to Stevenson, informing him that we had captured the elk, and asking him if he was willing to give up the bet without having it con-veyed to his house. He replied that he had learned of the capture, and that he cheerfully gave up the stakes without farther trouble.

This was the first grown elk that was caught alive on the waters of the Susquehannah. It was sixteen hands high; its horns were five and a half feet long, with eleven branches.

CHAPTER IV.

FACE OF THE COUNTRY.

THE first bottom above the first fork of Pine Creek is one and a half miles long, and is called the Fork bottom. On the east side of the creek, there is a mountain about a mile and a half high, presenting a perpendicular, rocky side along the river, from twenty to thirty feet high. On the west side of the creek is a bottom a mile long, called the Pine bottom. At the head of the Pine Bottom is a steep mountain. On the west side also was a creek about five miles long. Up this little creek was a favorite resort for game, such as bears, panthers, and deer. The first three miles from the mouth of the creek, the country is very rough, making a fit place for the abode of bears and panthers. This creek heads in a yellow pine plain, where there are large quantities of iron ore, and some suppose that stone coal is deposited there. A furnace to work the ore was built in 1812. The ore proved good, but the furnace went down in two years, in consequence of being too far from a farming country. Crossing over, you arrived at a small bottom, called Hamilton's. Proceeding on you arrived at Black Walnut Bottom. We then cross to an island called Boatman's Island, thence to what is called Boatman's Bottom, about two miles long, on the east side of the creek. In the center of this bottom, from the east, comes in a little creek, four or five miles long. Three miles up this creek is a mountain where you find a great number of bears dens, and places for the bears and panthers to live. Hunters often kill bears in their holes in the month of February, and sometimes panthers. The creek heads in the border of a white Pine country called Hemlock Bottom. Then from Hemlock Bottom cross over to what is called English Bottom, about 2½ miles long; then cross to an island called Comfort Wanderer's Island, then cross to a bottom on the west side half a mile in length. Here puts in a large stream called the Trout Run. At the mouth of this run are perpendicular rock, from thirty to fifty and a hundred feet in height. This run is eighteen miles in length, and five miles of it comes from a yellow pine, beech, maple, and chestnut country, leading to where elk used to live. The elk used to come from the head waters of Young Woman's Creek, Kettle Creek, and Sinemahoning. Young Woman's Creek empties into the west branch of the Susquehannah, about eighteen miles above the mouth of Pine Creek, Kettle Creek puts into the west branch about two miles above the mouth of Pine Creek.

About the head waters of these streams was the favorite range of elk, bears and deer. Elk and bears used to travel from Kettle Creek and Young Woman's Creek, and come down Trout Run, across Pine Creek, and up Mill Creek on the east side of Pine Creek, three miles from its mouth. The country is rocky; the elk and bears generally traveled up the south branch of Pine Creek, this being a good place for them to live. About fifteen or sixteen miles further we come to the head waters of Tioga river, and the elk would not go much further east in consequence of there being a settlement at an early day. There the elk would stay part of the winter and some times go back by Trout and Mill Runs, but not frequently. From the head waters of the Tioga to the Round Islands there were three elk licks. The elk in the winter season used to stay near the head waters of the streams, where feed was abundant. About April they would go to the smaller streams where the feed was earlier, and stay there until about the first of May. They would frequently go to Big Creek, where the mountains were high, and remain for some time. They would stay among the mountains during the season of breeding, until their young had obtained considerable size — say from the first of May until the end of June.

At this time large quantities of moss was to be found in the bottom of the river in the shoal places when the elk would come to the river in great droves to eat it; generally in the evening. Sometimes they would come in the day time, in droves of from thirty to forty, and could be seen by the hunters, feeding on moss. They would generally stay around the river until the middle of August, and if they went away, they would return in three or four days. Then they would go to the highlands, in the beech and maple woods, where the feed was more tender and budding.

They would keep near the salt licks in large droves: sometimes as many as forty could be seen together near a lick. I have endeavored to show how far the elk went east from Pine Creek. We will commence at Trout Run, and endeavor to describe the face of the country on the west side. The first Bottom above Trout Run on the west side is called Trout Run Bottom. The next is a mile and a half in length, called Sugar Bottom. Proceeding on, we arrive at Ned Huff's Bottom, at the head of which comes in a large creek, twelve miles long, called Ned Huff's Run. At the foot of Ned Huff's Bottom was a favorite crossing for bears. I have described the number of crossing places which were necessary in consequence of the hills putting in on both sides. In traveling up or down the stream on foot or horseback, we had to cross from bottom to bottom, and keep up the beach of the river, there being no road, the mountains put in so steep. In summer, when the water was very low, we could sometimes pass two or three of these bluff points by picking our way in the shallow water and on the stones. When the water was unusually high there was great danger from rattlesnakes which lay among the rocks. Each family possessed a canoe, and when the water was not too low we traveled in them up and down the river. During the winter when the streams were frozen, we traveled in sleighs. The following are some of the principal runways for bears and elk. From Ned Huff's Creek to the head of Long Bottom was a great runway for bears. From the head of Long Bottom to Cedar Run, which came in on the west side of Pine Creek, was three quarters of a mile. At its mouth were perpendicular rocks, from fifty to two hundred feet high, hanging directly over the creek. The nooks between the rocks were not more than four or five rods wide. On the lower side of the creek were rocks from thirty to forty feet high. Cedar Creek was thirteen or fourteen miles long. About seven miles up the creek was a fork called the West Branch, which headed toward Kettle Creek. Another branch called Tawnerstock Branch, headed a northeast course against Round Island. The elk would frequently go from the west side of Pine Creek to the Round Islands to drink and eat moss. When at the Creek they were on the trail that came from the Tioga River. They would leave Pine Creek and travel west to the Tawnerstock Branch, then to the head waters of Kettle Creek, and thence to Sinemahoning, the greatest elk country known. The train continues from

Sinemahoning on to the head waters of the Allegany River. The first of the head waters of the Allegany on the elk trail was called Potato Creek. The trail went still west to Stump Creek. On the head waters of Stump Creek were large numbers of elk, bears and deer. Stump Creek runs into the Allegany River eighty miles above Pittsburgh. Then the elk country and trail continues on the head waters of the Kenzua Creek. From Kenzua Creek the trail continues south to the head waters of Tionesta. I could not trace the elk trail any further south from Tionesta than sixteen miles, but bears and deer still went south. We then went north to the head waters of Kenzua, where the trail of elk continued west to the head waters of Tuneangwant. This river, as nearly as I can recollect, is eighteen or twenty miles long. It runs into the Allegany river twelve miles below Olean. One mile above the mouth of Tuneangwant was still an elk trail that went to Big Valley Creek in Cattaraugus county, New York. From the head waters of Big Valley to Cattaraugus Creek was from four to six miles. Cattaraugus Creek empties into Lake Erie twenty-eight miles southwest of Buffalo. This is as far west as I know elk to range. I came down the Alleghany river in the year 1815, and remained over night at an Indian house below Olean, near where this runway crossed the Allegany. I asked an Indian if he knew where there were any elk. He replied that they were very plenty on the west side of the river, and some few on the head waters of the Cattaraugus. I told him that I wished to catch a live elk that winter, and that I had caught three, each sixteen hands high. He told me that he did not believe this, as they were so large and powerful with such formidable horns that no white man or Indian dare encounter them.

We will now go back to the year 1799, when I was seventeen years of age, and explain how I became acquainted with all these runways, the art of elk-hunting, and the general appearance of the country. In the above year a company of men were sent out by William Ellis, Samuel Wallace, and Henry Drinker, of Philadelphia, to survey the land. They came up Pine Creek with a keel boat loaded with flour, pork, sugar, chocolate, tea, and all kinds of clothing for the men. When they arrived at my father's one of the hands was sick, and wished to go home, saying that he could not endure the hardships of the woods. The chief of the surveying company whose name was Harris, asked my father if he could supply him with a hand. My father said he would like to but he could not spare his two oldest sons; however, he had a son of seventeen who could be spared if he would answer the purpose. Mr. Harris asked me if I would go. I replied that I should be glad to, as I was anxious to go to the woods. We soon arranged our terms, when my father took me into the house and gave me some advice in regard to my new undertaking. He told me that if I should become separated from my companions to be careful and not get lost; however, if this should happen I should not go down stream, as the streams ran into the river forty or fifty miles apart, and I should be compelled to follow down until I reached the river. He also directed me to take particular notice when I saw an elk lick, or a place where elk were plenty, as any information on this point would be of service whenever we should wish to hunt. I was very much pleased with this last remark, as I was very fond of hunting. We started the next morning, and went up the river about twenty-one miles. We there unloaded the boats, and all hands proceeded to build a large house and cover it with bark. In two days we had it raised and covered, when we left a man named John Church, with two pack-horses, to finish it. We divided into three companies, each consisting of two men to carry chain, one to blaze, and one surveyor. I went with Mr. Harris, as chain bearer. We commenced on the east side of the stream, and surveyed back about sixteen miles. The following Sunday we laid by fifteen miles east of Pine Creek. Our pack-horse man came to us about twelve o'clock Monday with a supply of provisions for the following week. We surveyed northward for two days, then took a westerly course to Big Pine Creek, at a place called Round Islands, having been twelve days in the woods. Within this time I found three elk licks on our route. This was near the last of May. The elk were on the small streams, living on the new feed, and going toward Pine Creek to eat the moss. I then discovered where the elk crossed from the east to the west. I found that on the west side there were more indications of their going and returning, than on the east side.

At Round Islands our pack-horse man again brought us a supply of provisions. We then surveyed westward about fifteen miles. Here we made an encampment, and were again met by our pack-horse man with supplies. We then surveyed east to Pine Creek, near our block-house. We had then been out from our place of rendezvous about a month. We were joined at this point by the three other companies. One of our pack-horse men was anxious to change places with some one else, as he was not accustomed to the woods, and did not like to lie out alone for fear of wolves and panthers. Mr. Harris asked if any of the men in the company of surveyors was willing to pack. They all declined, when one named John Strawbridge asked me if I was not willing to take the post. I consented to try it for two or three weeks. On Monday all hands started from the camp and two companies went to the west side to survey. On Tuesday morning I took two horses loaded with provisions and started for the two companies on the west side of the river. I had to go about nine miles up the creek before I struck off to the west. I was to remain by the creek that night, on account of the pasturage it afforded the horses. About three o'clock in the afternoon I unloaded the horses, turned them out to feed, and made a fire. As I was seated by my fire, I heard a strange sound proceeding from something a short distance up the creek. It was now the last of June, the season for the elk to come to the creek and eat moss. I looked up and saw as many as twenty of them, about fifty rods above me. I let them feed quietly, not caring to disturb them. I ate my supper, looked to my horses, which were feeding on the blue grass, and then went to the river to look again at the elk. The stream was full of them, eating the moss and drinking. Twenty-two more had arrived, making in all forty-three.

In the morning after I had eaten my breakfast, I loaded my horses and started. When I had proceeded about half a mile up the stream, I found the pack-horse and elk trail which I was to take. About three rods from the creek, nearly the whole herd of elk I had seen the previous night were lying in the trail. When they saw me approaching they sprang up and ran on ahead, keeping the path and tearing up the ground as they ran along, for a mile and a half, when they turned off to the south and were soon out of sight. I went north until I struck the district line, which I kept for sixteen miles, when I encamped for the night, on the head waters of Kettle Creek, finding good pasturage for my horses. At night I was surrounded by wolves, which frightened the horses by their howlings so that they came close to the fire. I tied them near the fire, fearing they might become so frightened as to break away and run home. The next morning, after proceeding six or seven miles, I arrived about eleven o'clock at a corner where I was to meet the two parties of surveyors. Neither party had arrived, and I saw no pasture for the horses. When I had unloaded and made a fire I commenced searching for pasturage. At length I found, about three-quarters of a mile from the camp a small brook running through a swale, affording tolerable pasture, to which I led the horses. About dark one company of the surveyors arrived at the camp. The next day about noon, the other party came in, and we all remained there the following night. One of the chain bearers was unwell, and they wished me to carry the chain for him, and let him take my place with the pack-horses. I consented to the arrangement, and he returned to the blockhouse. In four days we had completed the surveying which we had anticipated would occupy a week, and accordingly had three days of leisure before the next Monday. We were now at the head waters of Kettle Creek, Cedar Run, and Sinemahoning, which was a good country, with abundance of elk and deer, and some bears. We all had fishing lines, and we determined to employ the first day of our leisure in fishing. My comrade and I descended Kettle Creek about seven miles. There I found on the east side of the creek in the side of the mountain a large elk lick, to which I gave the name of Rock Lick. It was very much resorted to by the elk. As we were returning we saw a trail leading to the northeast, which was as fresh and distinct as if cattle had been traveling there. We all met at our camp and had a mess of trout which would have suited the palate of an epicure, had it not lacked the addition of a little salt. As I had another day at my command I concluded to employ it in exploring the country in the vicinity of our camp to see if it was frequented by elk. I accordingly started down the creek, and in going four miles I discovered a great number of elk-paths. After proceeding four miles farther down the stream I arrived at a fork which had its source near the head waters of the Allegany River. I then returned to the camp, and supped again on trout, which some of our men had caught.

On Monday morning we commenced our final week's work of surveying, and completed it, as we had anticipated, on Saturday afternoon, at a place called Pine Island. We then started in pairs for our block-house. For a mile along the creek the rocks rose perpendicularly to the height of one, two and three hundred feet, and we were compelled to go two miles to the northward of our direct route. We then descended a sort of gully, picking our way along the rugged and broken rock, until we arrived within thirty feet of the bottom, when a perpendicular precipice presented itself. We crawled down the face of this by the crevices in its surface, until we reached a ledge about fifteen feet from the bottom. On the brow of this grew a beech sapling, and near it an iron-wood about ten feet high, with limbs nearly to the ground. My companion, John Strawbridge proposed to cut down the iron-wood sapling and trim off the limbs, leaving only a hook at the large end which we could attach to the beech sapling, to assist us down the rocks. We accordingly prepared our hook, when we disagreed as to who should first make the perilous descent. Strawbridge finally broke a couple of sticks and presented them to me, to draw one, and whoever had the longest should take the lead. I drew the longest cut, and prepared to descend. As I was passing down the pole, Strawbridge, who was holding the upper end of the pole, so that it should not slip off the beech sapling, looked over the brow of the ledge and saw a large rattlesnake coiled up in the exact spot where I would alight. He instantly called out to me, with an oath, to stop, as a rattlesnake lay coiled up beneath me. I was now about six feet from the top; to return was impossible, and it was with difficulty that I could maintain my position. I called to Strawbridge to throw the axe at the snake, which he did, and fortunately hit it so as to disable it. But a new calamity awaited me. A swarm of yellow wasps which were disturbed by our sudden intrusion upon their premises, came at me, striking me in my face and breast. I let go my hold and dropped to the ground, striking within three feet of the snake. Upon examination I found I was not much hurt, and I called to Strawbridge to come down. He refused, being afraid of the wasps. I looked around and found a long sycamore pole, which I cut, and placed against the rocks a short distance from where I had descended. He came down, and we started for camp, which was about four miles distant. When we arrived we found four companies of surveyors there. The next Monday morning, which was about the 5th or 6th of August, I was discharged and returned home. This was the last of my surveying, exploring elk countries and searching for elk-licks that year.

CHAPTER V.

IN the early settlement of the country, about the year 1792, the manner of life of the settlers, and the hardships and privations they were called upon to endure, rendered them capable of bearing up under fatigue and exposure, which those more tenderly reared would be unable to surmount. At that time, panthers, wolves, bears, elk, deer, and other wild animals filled the forest, and fish in great abundance, the streams. A person could go up the stream to where a dam had been built, and at any time with a hook and line could in an hour catch trout sufficient for a large family a day. Quite late one afternoon as I was fishing, I saw a great number of trout trying to jump over the dam. Two thirds of them succeeded in going over, but some of them would start too far away, and fall upon the dam, where I could catch them in my hands. While looking at them I contrived a plan for catching them, which was to set up a board about two feet in width, on the dam, to intercept them, and cause them to fall upon the dam. I at once set to work, and before leaving the place that night I placed boards the entire length of the dam. Early the next morning I took a basket and proceeded to the dam. My father asked me, as I was starting, where I was going. I replied that I was going to get some trout. He said that I had not time that morning, and that they did not want the fish. But I told him I would return in a short time; when I arrived at the dam I found as many as half a bushel of trout lodged on it. I filled my basket as quickly as possible, and hurried home. On my arrival there, my father expressing great surprise, inquired how I had caught so many. I informed him; and ever after, when the water was at a middle stage, we took in this way a great many; but when the water was high they could go over the dam. We caught eels in great numbers by lifting up the stones under which they were concealed, in the shallow part of streams. We speared a great many of them by night, in the following manner. Torches were made of yellow pitch pine, split fine, about seven feet in length, which threw a light so bright that we could see the fish on the bottom. We went up the stream to fish, as the eels kept on the bars and in the shallow water. My two older brothers and myself went together; I would draw the canoe, and they take the eels. Sometimes as we were out fishing, deer would come to the river to eat moss, within sight of us. When we saw them, we would all get into the canoe — one held the light, another sat in the forward part of the canoe, generally with two guns, and the third one sitting in the stern, would push the canoe along the stream as carefully as possible. Sometimes we could approach so near as to shoot them as they raised their heads erect to look at the light. Sometimes they would stand still long enough for the hunter to bring down a second one with the other gun. At other times they would start away, when we would wave the light, and as they ascended the bank they would become frightened at their shadows, thinking it was a wolf or panther, and run directly to the light, where they remained looking at it, till we could get another and perhaps two more shots at them. In this manner we would proceed up the stream from five to six miles, and in that distance we could often kill from two to four deer, and if the night was favorable we could catch from sixty to a hundred eels, besides a quantity of salmon, pike, and rock-fish. We would generally fish while passing up the stream, and hunt in passing down.

Fish and venison being so abundant in the vicinity where we lived, and very scarce at the mouth of Pine Creek, twenty-six miles distant, we used them as articles of traffic, and by exchanging them with inhabitants there, for wheat, rye, corn, buckwheat, salt, leather, and other necessaries, we obtained a supply of those articles. The night before we were to start, we would go up the stream from eight to twelve miles, and fire-hunt as we went down, arriving at home in the morning, just as the others had the load ready to start. We would then load in our fresh venison, and as the river was rapid, we could go down in time to dispose of our load and load for the return voyage before night. As we had to ascend against the rapid current, this was more difficult, taking two or two and a half days. Frequently in hunting, the bears and wolves would follow us for the entrails of the deer. Some times after killing a deer, we found it too lean to eat, when we would abandon it to the wolves and foxes, which we could hear howling and barking in our rear, guided by our fires. Occasionally a still more savage panther would rush in and drive these from their repast. When a deer was suitable for food we dressed it at once, and they were thus sure of obtaining the refuse.

After the first of October, the mode of taking fish was to make an oblique wall in the creek, letting it extend at the upper end about twenty feet, and come together at the lower end so near as only to admit the fish basket, which we made of laths and timber. It being in the center of the stream, the fish would mostly pass down between the walls and enter the basket. We generally built the wall where there was a slight rapid, leaving a fall of about eighteen inches at the basket, into which the fish would pass, and could not escape. The first season that my father constructed a basket, he took pattern by some of his neighbors below us. There came a rise of water about the last of October, and we caught but few fish that year. The next season he determined to put in a basket that would prove effectual whether the water was high or low. He commenced building in June, intending to be in season. He concluded to construct it differently from any he had seen. He made one wall shorter and at a sharper angle with the bank than the other, thus bringing his basket nearer the shore on which he lived, making it more easy of access, and left the lower ends of the walls about ten feet apart, enabling him to put in a large basket, and fastened the timbers so strongly under the wall that the basket stood there seven years. When winter came he let down the end of the basket and took off the sides, so that the ice could pass over it without injury. The next season, when we wanted to use it, we had only to raise the end and sides, and fasten the corners, and it was ready for use. At that time there were no boats or lumber rafts to run down, and only one family lived above us, eight miles distant, so we only left an opening in our wall for hunters to pass with their canoes. The second night after we had finished it was rainy, and upon such nights the eels played backward and forward over the ripples. In the morning my father went down to the basket, and found seven or eight large eels, and eight or ten salmon, with a quantity of suckers and other small fish. We found our basket to be very profitable from that time until the last of October. We were so abundantly supplied with fish from this source that we used them to feed our hogs, and found them very useful for that purpose, as we were compelled to keep them in our enclosure to protect them from wild animals. About the fifth of October, in that season, there came a rise of water in Pine Creek. The succeeding night we caught about two barrels of eels and three wagon loads of suckers. From this time we continued to take from twenty to thirty or forty eels besides a number of other fish nightly, until about the tenth of November, when there came another rise of water in the creek, and in three hours we took two barrels of good salmon and rock-fish, with four wagon loads of suckers. At dark the eels began to run, when my father, assisted by three of us boys and a man, began to carry out the eels, but the other fish came in so rapidly as to dam up the water, so that the eels would go over the sides of the basket and as they were difficult to catch, we threw out fish and eels to make room for the eels. Finding that we were losing many eels in this way, my brother brought the canoe, and placed it under the basket at a place where water did not come, and raked the eels back into it as they came. We made an opening in the basket, through which they fell, and we found the plan to work admirably. In about ten hours the river had risen so high as to overflow the basket, which put an end to our operations for that night. We had then carried out about twelve wagon loads of suckers, three barrels of eels and two barrels of salmon and rock-fish, besides throwing a great quantity out of the basket, to keep it from overflowing. We then built a good tight house of slabs, into which we put our suckers, and threw over it a large quantity of pine and hemlock boughs, to prevent their freezing. We fed our fattening hogs for the next three weeks upon fish, when we commenced feeding them corn, and at the end of the next four weeks the pork was equally as good as if fattened wholly on corn. We then kept three hogs through the winter on fish. Our supply lasted until about the middle of April. At that time, eels were worth in that country, from five to seven dollars per barrel, according to the demand. Salmon and other good fish were worth from four to six dollars a barrel. We estimated the fish fed to our hogs to be worth no more than seven or eight dollars as corn was very cheap at that time. If we had sold our fish at a very low rate, the four barrels of salmon, at five dollars a barrel, and five barrels of eels at seven dollars a barrel, and the fish we fed to hogs at eight dollars (besides, two months of the year we caught enough to supply the family all the time,) this would show the value of our fish basket for the first year. We estimated that the fish caught in it was worth to us, at the lowest rate, from sixty to seventy-five dollars, besides the supply for the family. The trout caught that season, which we kept for the family use, would have been worth twenty dollars more.

During the first few years of our residence here, we would often look up the creek in the morning, and see a deer, coming at the top of its speed, followed by three or four wolves — sometimes two on each side of the creek. We would immediately prepare and go out to meet them. Sometimes we captured the deer with very little trouble, but often the wolves would catch and spoil it before we came up. In this manner the wolves ran the deer from the first of July until the last of January. During the winter, when the river was covered with ice, the deer would fall into the air holes and become an easy prey. We took off the skin and if the deer did not prove to be very good, we would leave half of it to the wolves, but if it was good, we left the refuse parts to encourage them in pursuing the deer. Often while we were dressing deer the wolves would stand within twenty rods, howling most discordantly. We finally obtained a gun and dogs, and turned our attention to hunting. We commenced about the first of July, and continued until November. The wolves and dogs hunting together, sometimes one and sometimes the other obtaining the deer, and if it fell into our hands we always left the wolves their portion to keep them near, for we considered them of great assistance to us in hunting. As there was no bounty on wolves at that time, and we had no sheep for them to kill, we never destroyed them. They often aided us to three or four deer in a week. When we were fire-hunting, and had killed a deer, we often stopped to dress it, and left the wolves their portion, and if we had not the fortune to catch one, we would cach fish and leave them, to keep them in our vicinity. The howling of the wolves upon our track was generally mingled with the scream of wildcats, and often they would fight over the food we left them. Frequently when our dogs were chasing a deer the wolves would take it from them, and the dogs would sometime take one from the wolves in the same manner. The wolves and the dogs would often be in pursuit of the same deer, but when we were near enough, we could generally take it from them.

In the months of June and July we could often see from two to five hundred fish sunning themselves in the shoal water. The wildcats would stand watching them, and when they approached near enough to the shore, they would seize and bring out as many as three fish each, before they could escape. The black fox would sometimes dive in water two feet deep, and bring out fish. The red and silver tail foxes did not dive, but watched along the shore and took the fish in the same manner as the wildcats. We never killed them when we saw them fishing, as their skins were not as valuable then as in the fall and winter, but we would often shout and alarm them, to see them run. At the proper season, when their skins were good, we used to trap them. We began to trap foxes about the beginning of November, baiting with fish, which we found to be the best bait. We would roast an eel and trail it through the snow for some distance to the trap, and they would follow the scent. We found this to be the most successful manner of securing them.

CHAPTER VI.

DANGER FROM RATTLESNAKES.

THE first season of our residence there the snakes were so numerous that we used to clear the yard and build fires around the house to keep them away. We were careful to have the house made very tight to prevent their entrance, and we closed the door early in the evening in the summer, and did not open it until day-light in the morning for fear of them, they were so numerous. Before we commenced making fires around the house in the morning, we frequently found the snakes lying in the yard near the house. One morning quite early, as my father was leaving the house, he heard a hiss like a goose nearly over his head. He paid no attention to it, however, and on his return he cast his eyes up over the door, and discovered a large rattlesnake lying directly over his head, hissing and darting its tongue toward him. He killed the snake and went into the house much alarmed, saying that he should leave that place, as he feared we would all be bitten by the rattlesnakes. About three days afterward, the hired man went on the roof of the house to repair it, he found a large rattlesnake in quiet possession, seeing which he was terribly alarmed, and jumped to the ground. I then went to the roof and destroyed the snake. On leaving the house we always put on a pair of woolen socks and leggins over our shoes to protect our legs from the snakes; this was a necessary precaution for many years. Burning the woods proved of some benefit to us, as the snakes would not come near a place where a fire had been, for some time. About the first of August they came in pairs, and should one be killed, the other would be found at the end of even three or four days near the dead one. Sometimes toward the end of August, thirty or forty could be seen at one time lying on and among the rocks. My brother and myself were hunting and fishing one afternoon, and as we were pushing up the river in our canoe we passed a rattle-snake's den, near which we counted forty rattle-snakes, some coiled up, and others stretched out, sunning themselves. We went ashore and provided ourselves each with a stick made similar to a flail, so that we could kill them with a single blow. One then went below them and the other above, and we killed all we could until we met. We succeeded in killing thirty of the forty snakes which we first counted. In killing so many snakes, we inhaled so much of the poisonous effluvia as to make us sick. We returned home immediately and took freely of sweet milk and hog's lard, to prevent any more serious effects. Frequently when hunting we saw eight or ten snakes, but we would only kill four or five of them nearest us, or that were ugly. We never found them numerous at a greater distance than three miles from the river, and there they were near a brook or small stream. The country from near the mouth of Pine Creek extending several miles up to a place called the Big Elk Lick, was a great resort for them. Within this distance there were six rattlesnake dens. The first den was on the east side of the creek, near Clark's Bottom. Up the creek, about nine miles above Clark's Bottom, was another. About two miles farther, at Black Walnut Bottom, was a small island of about two acres, where we always found great numbers of them. Still farther up the creek, about nine miles from the last place, lying in the river, about twelve feet from the nearest shore was a rock about forty feet long by fifteen wide, called Rattle-snake Rock. On this the snakes would often lie in piles. On the opposite side of the river was another seventy feet long and twenty wide, on which could often be seen forty snakes at a time.

In the year 1794, James King and a Mr. Manning went on an exploring expedition up Pine Creek, to ascertain if any elk were to be found, and also if any Indians were in the neighborhood. They went up the stream above Big Meadows. When about twenty miles up the creek, they found the rattlesnakes so numerous that they were compelled to anchor their canoe in the middle of the stream to avoid them. The first night they built a fire on shore, and before morning three snakes made their appearance. They then concluded it would be more safe in the canoe. About the third day they arrived at the larger rock on the west side of the river, and found as many as thirty rattlesnakes lying on the rock, sunning themselves. They pushed their canoe to the other shore, and when passing the smaller rock, they discovered on the top a pile of rattle-snakes as large as an out-door bake-oven. They lay with their heads sticking up in every direction, hissing at them. Proceeding up the river a short distance, they could see, as they approached the shore, snakes lying where they intended to land. They therefore continued on a mile and a half to a thicket of hemlock, which they knew the snakes would not approach, and accordingly went ashore and prepared dinner. About one mile and a half farther they arrived at the second fork of Pine Creek. Here they saw about forty elk drinking in the creek, and as far as they could see they discovered elk in the stream. They estimated that there were nearly two hundred elk at the creek. The next day they pushed up the creek about eleven miles, when they came to the Round Islands, on the shore opposite which was a den of rattle-snakes, about a quarter of a mile back from the creek, in a rocky place. It being in the month of August, when the snakes always come to the water, they saw in a space of twenty rods as many as sixteen rattle-snakes, all about a rod from the water. Not wishing to land in such company, they proceed up the creek half a mile to a hemlock thicket, where they landed and prepared supper. They then dropped out into the stream, and anchored for the night. But they found troublesome neighbors on the water, as well as on land. The gnats were so numerous and annoying that it was impossible to sleep. They accordingly laid pieces of bark across the canoe, covered them with clay, and built upon it a fire of rotten wood. This raised a smoke which protected them effectually. The next day, about eight miles further up the creek, they arrived at the third fork of Pine Creek. On the west side, opposite the fork, they discovered a large tract of cleared land, consisting of as many as a hundred and sixty acres, to which they gave the name of the Big Meadows. They were the first white men ever there. It had been cleared by the Six Nations, and they thought had probably been vacated for twenty or thirty years, but they could still discern marks of corn-hills. A few hickory trees grew next the river and along the foot of the hill, but besides these not a tree or shrub was visible, and it was covered with blue grass. On the opposite side of the creek, near the fork, they found a plum orchard of twenty acres, abounding with fruit. Between the plum orchard and the creek was a tract of cleared land of about thirty acres, which appeared to have once been a corn-field. In this vicinity they found a great many elk and bears. As it was not the season for the latter, and their fur and skins were of no value, they did not molest them. They then ascended the fork seven miles, when they arrived at a place which they called Big Marsh. Here the country was more level, and less rocky than it was down Pine Creek. From here they returned to the Meadows, where they left their canoe, and proceeded on foot twelve miles up the creek, where they found a very large elk lick, and saw about sixty elk at the creek, at one time. They killed one elk, and the others became frightened at the report of the gun, and fled. When they had killed and dressed the elk, one of them proceeded about a mile further, and found an Indian camp, that appeared to have been occupied by as many as eight or ten persons, but few days previous. On his return to his companion, he informed him of the discovery he had made, and they concluded to return. They started accordingly, going down the creek five miles to a small stream which they ascended two miles, and encamped for the night. The next morning they went to their canoe by a different course, and descended the creek to the second fork. After exploring, for two days, the country lying on the second fork, they proceeded down the creek twelve miles to a place called Hamilton's Bottom, and the following day arrived at the town of Jersey Shore, which terminated their expedition. They were hired by a company in Philadelphia to explore the country for the purpose of locating land-warrants, and were the first white men that ever penetrated the wilderness lying on Pine Creek and its tributaries. The information which thy obtained was of great importance to us when we first settled in this country, as it enabled us to find where and how the elk lived, where the dens of rattle-snakes were, and how to avoid them. When hunting the elk we frequently went to the dens of rattle-snakes to see how many were visible at once. We used to burn the woods in May to destroy the snakes; and another mode was to make a large pile where they were the most numerous, and toward evening set fire to it, when the snakes would run into the fire, and vent their impotent rage upon it, until they were burnt to death. I hunted five years in this part of the country, and in all that time I noticed that the rattle-snakes were never seen farther than six miles from Pine Creek, and on the smaller streams they were never seen more than two miles from the waters. They were never found near the source of the small streams. I have taken particular notice of the habits of the snakes, while hunting on various streams.

In the year 1816, I resided near Cornplanter's Town, on the Allegany River. I made inquiries of Cornplanter, then the head chief of the Six Nations, concerning the rattlesnake, and he told me that thirty years previous they had found the snakes as numerous from the place called Red Bank to the State line, as they used to be at Pine Creek. He said all the traveling in summer had to be done in canoes, on account of them. The way they destroyed them was to burn the woods in the same manner that we did. I asked him if any of the people were ever bitten. He replied that the men were seldom bitten as they wore woolen socks and leggins, but several of the women and children had been bitten, and it proved fatal in some cases before remedies could be procured. When they were obliged to lie out at night in a place which was infested by snakes, they drove four crotches into the ground, upon which they placed poles, and across these they laid pieces of bark. In this manner they avoided sleeping on the ground. In summer they always kept a fire around the place where they slept, to protect themselves while asleep. I asked Cornplanter where he thought the bears, elk, deer and panthers were the most plenty thirty years previous. He answered that in the year 1786 he found the deer more plenty from the State line to Red Bank, and about twelve miles back from the river, than they were on Pine Creek. But he thought bears were not as plenty, and that panthers were quite numerous on Kenzua Creek and the Tionesta and the country between the head waters of those streams and the Susquehannah river. Elk, he said were not as plenty on the Allegany as they were on Pine Creek; and beaver, otter, and other animals valuable for their fur, he had found more abundant on the Susquehannah than on the Allegany. Bears were found in great numbers from the mouth of Conewango Creek to Chautauque Lake. They had a crossing place where they passed from the head waters of the Tionesta to the lake. He said his two sons, Henry and John O'Bayle, killed in one summer, fifteen bears on the banks of Chautauque Lake.

Soon after our conversation I again saw Cornplanter and he told me that he had learned, by a letter from the Presbyterian Society, of Pittsburgh, that they intended to send a preacher to establish a school at Cornplanter's Town, and he asked me to send my children, as there was no school or place of instruction near us. I told him that when they sent the minister and teacher, I would give him an answer. In about two weeks the teacher arrived. He was from Virginia, and his name was Samuel Oldham. He was accompanied by his wife. They were both pious people and members of the Presbyterian Church. A man by the name of George Hilderbrand came with them as interpreter. He had lived for several years among the Indians on the Allegany, and understood the language. After the teacher had been here about two days, a man by the name of Walter Seaman and myself went to see him and Cornplanter about sending our children to their school. Cornplanter said he did not know as they would be willing to teach our children without pay, but he would be willing to do his part, as he thought it would be an assistance in teaching their children to speak the English language. He said that the minister was expected to arrive the next Saturday evening, and preach to them on the next Sabbath, and they could then ascertain whether we would be permitted to send our children to their school. I asked of Cornplanter the reason why the Quakers left them about four years previous. He said the Quakers did not keep the Sabbath, and he thought that was very wrong; and they taught the children that he was no wiser or better than any other man, and ought not to be considered so. This displeased him very much, as he wished to be considered the wisest and best of his tribe, and he told the Quakers that they might go, as the tribe did not wish to have them on their ground, or to have their children taught in that manner. About four years before this the oldest Indians removed into Cattaraugus County, New York. I asked him if he did not regret to have them all leave him. He replied that he was not sorry to have them go, as they were better situated on their own land, and the young men who were left would soon be grown up to take the places of those who had gone. He also said that they were not willing to be ruled by him, and he was quite willing that they should leave. He asked me what I thought of the Quakers. I said that I liked them very much, as they were a very sober people, and did not drink or swear. He did not coincide with me in my favorable opinion of them.

In the year 1817, as Cornplanter with his son and myself were going down the river in a canoe from the state of New York, where we had been at work, I inquired of his son, Henry O'Bayle, if his father would be willing to talk about the wars and battles in which he had been engaged.

On being questioned, he replied that it was a subject upon which he was fond of conversing. I asked him what was the first battle he was ever engaged in. He replied that it was at Braddock's defeat. He was then seventeen years of age, and engaged with the French and Indians against the British. He said that there were about six thousand Indians, and some few French. He supposed there were about double the number of Indians that there were of white men. He returned, after the battle, to his own place of residence. There was a smaller number of Cornplanter's own tribe, than of any other tribe then present. They had intended, in case they were victorious, to continue their march to Philadelphia, driving the whites before them, and compel them to quit the country. But when the battle was over and the plunder was divided, they became insubordinate and could no longer be kept in order. The original plan was therefore abandoned. On his return, Cornplanter informed his tribe of the dissensions in their army and said, that in their then divided state it was useless to contend longer against the British, and they had better make peace with them as soon as possible. His advice, however, was not followed. I asked him if he was ever on the Susquehannah. He laughed and asked if any of my friends had ever been killed there. I answered in the negative. He then asked if the people on the west branch of the Susquehannah did not entertain feeling of enmity against him. I replied that nothing was cherished against him; that whatever acts of hostility he had committed were undoubtedly instigated by the British, and upon them, therefore, rested the blame. He said this was true; that the British supplied them with ammunition and paid them for scalps. I asked him how many men had fallen by his own hand. He said he had killed seven. I asked him if his half brother was not killed there, to which he answered that he was, in an attack upon a block-house, at Munsee hill, and that he was present himself. I asked him if he remembered whether they intended to set fire to the block-house. He made no reply to this, but asked if I or any of my friends were there. I told him that I was not there, being but a boy at that time, nor had I friends there, but that I knew the man who shot his brother; his name was Armstrong. I also knew another man, by the name of Carr, who was in the block-house, and who now lived within ninety miles of Cornplanter. Armstrong, Carr and two others, were the only ones in the block-house at the time of the attack.

CHAPTER VII.

WOLF AND BEAR HUNTING.

THE following is the manner in which wolves were hunted during the early years of our residence in the country. Early in May they were found near the heads of streams, either among the rocks or in hollow logs. When they were near, the hunter generally found paths which were formed by the old she-wolf in passing to and from her den. If none were visible, he imitated the howl of a wolf, to which the old one, if within hearing, would reply, and thus betray her retreat. If not successful in one place, he continued his search from the head of one stream to another. Some times they were found a mile or two from the head of a stream, if there was any convenient place for them to den. Occasionally the hunter could kill a deer, when he hung up different parts of it where it would be found by the wolves, and if upon his return, they had been taken, he felt sure there were wolves in the vicinity. He would then imitate the howl of a wolf, which would be answered if any wolves were within hearing. If the young ones were found in the absence of the dam, great care was used to leave no indications of any one having been at the den. If the hunter had no trap, he would climb a tree and wait the approach of the old wolf. About the first of December was the best time for baiting them with meat, as the old ones weaned their young at that season, and the latter were scattered over the woods. The wolf generally has from five to ten puppies. The meat was sometimes roasted and dragged over the trail for thirty or forty rods before baiting the trap with it. The most favorable time for trapping wolves was during rainy weather, as the rain would obliterate the scent of the trapper. When there was no rain, it was customary to carry along a pail of water, and sprinkle on the tracks for the same purpose. When the hunter had his traps set, he would climb into a tree and howl like a wolf until they collected near, when they would get into the traps, or he could shoot them from his retreat. The month of February was another favorable time for taking them, as it is the season for them to mate, when they collect in great numbers. They can be easily taken in traps at this season, as they are very ravenous, and will run any hazard for the sake of the meat with which the trap was baited. Another successful manner of taking them was in what was called wolf-houses, which were constructed in the following manner. A favorable place was found on the steep side of a hill, in a place frequented by wolves in passing from one stream to another. In the side of the hill a hole was dug so deep that the upper side would be on a level with the roof of the house. In this hole the house, about ten feet square, was built and the same in height, of beech and maple logs. The top covered with heavy logs, leaving a hole five feet one way by two and a half the other. Into this a trap door is fitted, with a spring underneath. The bait is placed in such a position that the wolf, to reach it, must step upon the trap-door, when it drops down and precipitates the animal to the bottom, when it springs back to its place. If a female is the first to fall into the trap, the others will keep running about over the trap door, and one after another will fall in, until the greater part of the whole pack is caught. The house is built several months before the season for its use, to accustom them to it.

About the first of September the wolves commenced running deer into the river. This is another favorable season for hunting them. When we saw a deer running and no dog in sight, we were sure it was pursued by wolves. If we wished to save the deer for our own use, we shot it before it was overtaken by the wolves. We then let the deer lie some time, and if the wolves were not too much frightened by the report of the gun, they would come up to the deer, when we could perhaps kill two or three of them. This is always done early in the morning, and the wolves lie still the rest of the day. When I was a young man, steel traps were scarce and dear, and we were compelled to invent substitutes which would be unnecessary at the present day.

Bears were hunted and caught by us in the following manner. About the first of May they could be found at the streams, turning over the stones along the shore in search of fish with which to feed their cubs. The hunter had to exercise great care to keep where the wind would not blow from him to the bear, as the latter would detect the slightest taint of his presence. After killing the old one he could some times take the cubs, but if they ran he concealed himself and they would return in a short time. If he failed to approach near enough to kill the bear, he let his dogs after her, and she would soon climb a tree, followed by her cubs, when he shot the old one from the tree, and then withdrew with his dogs until the cubs descended and gathered around their dam. If he found it difficult to take them, he could set traps or snares for them, as they will linger near their dam for two or three days.

Another manner of taking bears was in houses, similar to those used for wolves. They were made larger, being generally ten by fourteen, and built upon a floor of large logs, unless a large flat rock could be found in a convenient place to build upon. The top was covered with logs or rocks, so heavy that the bears could not raise them. The door was in the side, and hung at the top. When ready for use, the door was swung up and the bait connected with it by a rope, in such a manner that the bear when it pulled upon the bait, would loose the fastening, and cause the door to fall down to its place, and fasten the bear into the house. In this manner we sometimes caught the old bear and cubs at once. When they were secured in this manner, we could convey them home alive in the following manner. The eyes were covered, and the mouth muzzled. A rope was attached to each foot, and one around the neck; to the neck was also fastened a pole twenty feet long, and another rope forty feet long, to which a horse was attached. A man then went ahead holding the pole and two behind, holding the ropes, to prevent the bear from going too rapidly. When the weather was warm and the bear fat we had to go very slowly. To tame them we used to attach a horse to them and lead them around. If they were stubborn and not easily tamed, we shut them up and fattened them for their oil, which was valuable.

About the last of July and first of August, when berries were ripe, was a good season for taking bears, either in bear-houses or by shooting them. They were most plenty where there were whortleberries; if they could find no whortleberries, they would eat blackberries, and if there were neither, they could be found where there were wild cherries. If not successful in taking them by means of bear-houses, the hunter pursued them with dogs. When he came within sight of one he let the dogs loose, when the bear would climb a tree, before running a great distance. If the tree was so high that the bear could not be reached without much difficulty, the hunter retired a short distance and waited until it came down, when he would drive it up another. If he was prepared with ropes, he could capture it alive. My first experience in catching bears was in 1805, in the following manner. As a large party of young men and women were out picking whortleberries we discovered a bear eating berries. Having eight or ten good dogs with us, we thought it was a fine chance for sport, and accordingly gave chase. In a short time he ascended a tree, but it was too high for our purpose, and we withdrew until he came down, when we forced him up another. We continued in this manner driving him from one tree to another, until we had him up one about fifteen feet to the lower limb. One of the young men proposed to take the bear alive, but another said it could not be done; but I concurred in the opinion of the first, and we began laying a plan to accomplish it. In the first place we peeled bark, with which we made ropes, with a noose in the end of each. We then made a scaffold by the tree, upon which one of the party stood, and with a pole slipped a noose over the neck and another over the fore paws of the bear. We now had him in our power, and drove him down the tree nearly to the ground. We then tied a pole across his neck, each end of which was taken by a man, and in this manner we drove him a couple of miles, when we concluded he had given us sufficient amusement, and cutting the ropes set him at liberty. Bears from six months to three years old can easily be taken in this manner, but the old ones are not so easily managed. During the months of January and February was a favorable time for taking bears by tracking them to their dens. When the hunter had found the den, he approached it, well prepared with dogs and guns, and threw in burning sulphur, which soon started them out. They could then be shot as they emerged from the hole. It was necessary to be well prepared, as the bears are very ferocious at this season, and it would be a perilous adventure for one to rouse them without plenty of dogs and guns. As many as five were sometimes found in one den, but there was not generally more than one.

CHAPTER VIII.

ANOTHER ELK HUNT.

In December, 1811, I went to Lycoming county, for the purpose of catching a live elk. The hunting ground was in the vicinity of Pine Creek. I was accompanied by my brother Benjamin, then seventeen years of age, and three men whom I had hired to assist me. On the 8th we started, each man carrying a knapsack with provisions for a week. We also took ropes sufficient to hold an elk. We ascended Pine Creek about fifteen miles to a place called the Lower Round Islands. Here we left the creek and climbed a hill, the summit of which was two miles from the base. After traveling in a westerly direction about two miles we struck the track of three elk. We supposed, from their freshness, that they were made the evening previous, and by bucks. We followed the track about a mile and a half, when we came up with them, and they wheeled and gazed at us. We had four dogs with us, two of which we let loose. The elk started and ran about four miles and then turned and fought the dogs until we came up. We then fired to encourage the dogs, when they singled out one of them, and attacked him furiously. He took a westerly course, with both dogs after him, while the two others went to the north. We pursued the one the dogs were after. He ran about eight miles, and then turned upon the dogs, which soon tired out and came back, meeting us about four miles from where they had fought. We continued on, and encamped near where the elk had stood at bay. The next morning we followed the elk about three-quarters of a mile, and came to where he had left his westerly course and turned to the south. About half a mile farther we came to where he had been feeding, and had lain during the night, and discovered him about fifty or sixty rods ahead of us. We let the two fresh dogs go, and they approached within a few yards of him before he saw them. He then started, running about six miles, when he turned to fight the dogs, tired them out, and they returned to us. We continued on, however, to the place where the elk had turned upon the dogs. As it was a very blustering day, and there was good camping ground, we halted for the night. All of the hired men now became discouraged. They said that our dogs were worthless for elk-hunting, that they had gone thus far without accomplishing any thing, and would probably not if we continued the chase; and that they were tired and wished to return home. I told them that the direction in which the elk was then traveling led toward home, and it was as well to follow the track as to take any other course. Also, that as they had engaged for an indefinite period, they were under obligations to remain with me, if I desired it, until we had caught a live elk. The next morning they concluded to continue, and we started after the elk. We went two miles and found where he had been feeding. A short distance farther we saw him lying down. All the dogs were then let loose, when they pursued the elk very closely, and the whole party of us ran about four miles, whooping and shouting with all our might, when we met the dogs returning. The men were again discouraged, and desired to go home. I told them they were now going toward home, and they might as well continue. Some harsh words followed, when I told them it was my business whether they went home or not, and that I should not consider myself bound to pay them if they did not remain with me until I had secured an elk. They then concluded to go on, and we followed the track about six miles, and arrived at a high mountain, with steep, rocky sides, and within two miles of the place from which we started, between Cedar Run and Big Pine Creek, at the mouth of the former stream. From there the elk took a westerly course again. On the side toward Pine Creek many of the rocks rose two or three hundred feet perpendicular. From appearances, we judged that the elk had been on the rocks, awaiting the dogs, and this would have been a capital chance to secure him, if the dogs had kept up the chase. The men, thinking that the elk had departed from the homeward course, wanted to leave the track. I had been there before, and knew where we were, but they were totally unacquainted with the place. I pointed to the rocks and said, " If you wish to go down the sides of that mountain and take a chance of finding your way home, go; I shall keep on the track."

[43]

But they concluded to follow me, and we again started in
pursuit of the elk. We went about six miles, to the east
branch of Cedar Run, in the forks of which we encamped
for the night. The next morning we proceeded about a
mile and a half, to the west branch of Cedar Run, where
we discovered the elk feeding. I told them to keep the
dogs quiet, and we would drive him up the hill, the summit of which was about a mile distant. We followed him
about half a mile, when I told them to let loose all four of
the dogs, and to encourage them by firing a gun. The elk
then ran directly south about five miles, and turned to
the east. We walked on quite briskly. I told them that
the elk was going toward a famous elk-crossing, about six
miles distant, and half a mile from our starting-point, called
Black Walnut Bottom. This seemed greatly to encourage
them, and they pushed on, anticipating a speedy return home.
About a mile and a half farther, the elk ran toward a rock
which rose about two feet above the surface of the ground,
and was about twenty-five by forty feet on the top, but
for some unaccountable reason, turned away and passed on.
The nice scent of the dogs, however, enabled them to detect the cause at once, and they left the track of the elk,
and commenced barking furiously around a hole in the center of the rock. Two of the men, Francis and Fleeharty,
were in advance of me and when they arrived at the rock,
they sent all the dogs down the hole. In a short time a
bear made his appearance at the surface. The men drove
it back, but it still endeavored to force its way out as often
as they kicked it back. I heard their shouts, and ran to
them, leaving two others behind with the gun. Soon after
I arrived the bear retreated to his cave, and we listened,
expecting to hear a struggle between him and the dogs. We
were not disappointed, for in about ten minutes we heard
the barking of the dogs, and soon one of them rushed out
as fast as possible. Very soon another followed, and then
the two others came bounding out. The bear stuck his
nose again out of the hole, and I jumped upon his head
with both feet, knocking him back, and called to the men
to give me a club. While speaking I observed that Francis
had an axe upon his shoulder, but was so much excited that
he was not aware of it. The bear once more made his appearance, and I asked Francis to give the axe to me. But
he called to me to stand out of the way, and giving the
bear a glancing stroke, the axe slipped from his hands and

went rattling down the hole. We then kicked the bear back, and kept him there, until the rest of the party came up with the gun. Upon trial I found that it was wet, and would not go off. I dried the pan and a second time attempted to shoot, but with no better success. I then picked out the caked powder, put some priming into the pan, and told the men to stand back. The bear soon came to the top of the hole, but paused upon seeing so many of us in the vicinity. I fired into his mouth, and the bullet broke his neck bone. He fell back, slid down the hole, gave a heavy plunge, and all was silent. Our next object was to bring our booty out to the surface. None of us wished to enter the den, yet we were not willing to leave it there. We finally concluded to decide it by drawing cuts, and the longest two were drawn by Fleeharty and myself. We drew again, to decide which should take the lead, and the lot fell upon Fleeharty. A rope was placed around his waist, and taking a torch in his hand, he started and I followed, leaving orders with those above not to raise the rope until I called. After descending obliquely about thirty feet, we arrived at a precipice of about three feet, at the bottom of which lay the bear on its back. The fears of Fleeharty magnified into a live bear each foot of the dead one, as it lay in the flickering light of his torch, and, thinking he had at least four bears to encounter, he screamed, " Pull me up! " I quieted him, and taking the torch from his hands, and peering down into the hole, I discovered the cause of Fleeharty's alarm. I told him what I saw, and requested him to proceed, but he could not muster courage enough to descend the precipice, and I pushed him off, following myself. As he struck the bottom, the torch fell from his hands, and he set up a scream of, " Murder! Murder! " " Pull me up! " " The bears are after me! " I picked up the torch and showed him that all his panic was caused by one dead bear. We then commenced exploring the cave, and found it to be quite a curiosity. The room was, as I judged about twelve by eighteen feet in size, and seven or eight feet high. The ceiling was very smooth, with right-angled corners, and on two adjacent sides were projections like seats about eighteen inches high, and fifteen wide, regularly formed, with well-defined angles. They extended the entire length of their respectives sides, while on the opposite sides was no such formation, or traces of any. Every thing had an artificial appearance. I called to those above to come down, and make further researches. In the northwest corner was an opening five feet high and three wide, which led to another regularly formed room, eleven by sixteen feet, but without seats or any thing remarkable. In the northwest corner of this room was an opening three feet by two, which led into a long narrow passage. We entered and proceeded about three rods, when our light began to burn dimly, and the thought occurred to me that there might be half a dozen bears or panthers concealed within, and if one should meet us in that narrow passage, our situation would be neither safe nor pleasant. I told the others my fears, and we accordingly returned to the large room. As we concluded that we could not find more comfortable quarters, we made arrangements to stay there all night. From the moss, leaves and branches which we found there, we supposed the bear must have made this rock his habitation for many winters — perhaps a dozen. We gathered some of the larger branches, and brought some dry wood from the outside, with which we made a large and cheerful fire. In a short time the smoke filled the room so densely that we were nearly suffocated, before we could gather up our implements and leave the place. It was now nearly dark, and a cold blustering night. There was no pine or hemlock in that region, with which to build a shanty, and we stretched blankets across poles and made a tent. We then built a fire, and as the ground was covered with snow, we procured bark and brush to lie on. When everything was prepared we ate our supper and went to sleep. The next morning after eating breakfast, we went to the rock, to take out our bear. Two of us entered the cave and tied a rope around the neck of the bear. The three men on the outside pulled on the rope, while we pushed, but we could not raise it over the ledge. We then cut a pole about twenty feet long, which we used as a lever, and by this means drew him out. We estimated that he weighed between four and five hundred. We then skinned it, tried out the oil, and cut up the meat. One of the party took the skin, and as much of the oil as he could carry, and each of the others took thirty or forty pounds of meat. The rest we hung about twelve feet from the ground, between two trees. We were then about three and a half miles from home. We started again on the elk-track, and kept it about two and a half miles, arriving at the top of a high hill, within sight of home. From there the elk turned to the northeast, when I told my companions

they might go home, but I continued on the track for about
two miles, when the elk crossed the creek. I then left the
track and went home. When I arrived there I found all
my hands seated around the fire, talking about my elk-
hunting abilities. All but my brother Benjamin said that
I could not catch an elk. They said that I was not like
my father, but more like other men, and all of my attempts
to catch a live elk would be vain. My brother, however,
insisted that I could catch one. I told them that I was
not so discouraged but that I should try again. I then sent
my brother to a place about twenty-five miles distant to
procure a man and good dogs, and some articles that I wanted, and told him to join me with them at a place fifteen
miles up the creek. I went to another brother who lived
three miles distant, and told him that I wanted him to assist me in hunting, and that I would give him the hides
of all that we should kill, but if we should succeed in taking one alive, I would pay him for his time and trouble.
He consented to go, and said that another man by the name
of Blackwell, who lived some eight or nine miles above,
had a good elk dog, and would be glad to accompany me
on the same terms. We drove up there with a horse and
cutter, and engaged Blackwell. We started from there with
a two-horse sleigh and a supply of provisions, going to
what was called the Lower Round Islands, where we encamped for the night, and sent back our team. The next day
we started on a westerly course, and after proceeding about
five miles, we found some old elk-tracks. They were so
full of newly-fallen snow that we could scarcely distinguish
them, and could only determine their direction by digging
out the snow and examining them. After satisfying ourselves on that point, we followed the tracks about three
miles, when we found a fresh track. The elk was going
toward the east, and I remarked that he would probably
cross at the Upper Round Islands, if we did not catch him
first. After following the track about three miles we arrived at a small hollow surrounded by rocks, with abundance of timber. As it was nearly night, and the weather
cold and stormy, we concluded to cut some hemlock boughs
and make a shanty. The next morning we started again
on the elk-trail, and after proceeding about two miles, we
found where he had been feeding. I went on ahead to re-
connoiter, and had gone but a short distance when I discovered him resting, chewing his cud. When the rest of

the party came up, I directed them to loose two of the dogs, of which we had three very good ones. The elk sprang up and started off toward Lower Round Islands with the dogs in full pursuit. When we arrived at the bluff overlooking the creek, he halted upon a large rock on the brow of a precipice of four hundred feet. From the lower side a large fragment had been disengaged, and torn a path forty feet wide and a mile long, to the creek, where it lodged, and stuck about fifteen feet out of the water, which was eight or ten feet deep. When I arrived I did not think it prudent to rope the elk there, fearing he would jump off and kill himself. I accordingly returned to the others, to prevent their approaching so near as to frighten him. We passed by him as cautiously as possible, built a fire and called off the dogs. We thought that the elk would then come off himself, during the night. Blackwell and my brother, however, became impatient, and wanted to see the elk. I consented but desired them not to disturb him, and to return soon. When they came within sight of the elk, Blackwell observed that there was a good chance to rope him, and my brother consented to try. They slipped the noose over his head without much difficulty, with the aid of a pole. They then attempted to draw the noose tight, and at the same moment the dogs seized the elk in the rear, when he sprang with one of the dogs clinging to him, down the precipice. At a distance of four hundred feet, he struck upon a sheet of ice which had been formed by water falling from the rocks above, from which he bounded, and slid seven hundred feet, stopping in a snow-bank, four hundred feet above the creek, three hundred of which was a sheet of frozen snow, and below that a perpendicular precipice of one hundred feet. I heard the plunge and suspected the truth. The men soon returned, and I asked what was the matter. They answered evasively, saying that they were sorry for what had happened. I told them my suspicions, and they acknowledged that they were true. I took it good-humoredly, as it could not now be helped, and told them we had better go after him. We started accordingly, going north about a mile, and came to a brook that ran down through the rocks, the bed of which we followed down to the creek. We then descended the creek three quarters of a mile and encamped under a projecting rock. My brother remained to build a fire, while Blackwell and myself went farther down to find, and if possible, to get the elk. We soon saw his hind quarters projecting out of the snow bank far above us. We followed a ravine which led obliquely up the steep bank to a large rock which had arrested the impetuous descent of the elk, and above which he now lay. On the rock stood a sapling, over which we threw a rope by attaching a stone to one end. When we had secured the rope, we resorted to our usual method of deciding which should take the lead, as we both shrunk from the perilous enterprise of scaling the rock by the aid of a slender rope, with nothing but a steep expanse of frozen snow between us and the brow of a precipice of one hundred feet. The lot fell upon Blackwell, and sticking the tomahawk in his belt, he went up. He then cut steps in the snow to the elk, which lay about forty feet above the sapling. I followed him, but believing the steps to be too small and unsafe, I requested him to slip the tomahawk down to me that I might enlarge them. One false step would have precipitated me down the crust of snow and over the precipice. I reached the elk safely, and we began to dig away the snow from the lower side, intending to roll it out upon the crust and let it slide down the snow bank. But Blackwell noticed that the sapling stood in the course it would take and feared that it would go with such force as to break it if he should hit it, and thus cut off our means of returning. I called to my brother to bring a pole with which to guide the elk, and then rolled it out upon the crust. It flew down the snow, giving the sapling a glancing stroke, and over the precipice striking the ice below with a heavy plunge. We retraced our steps and arrived safely on the ice. The meat of the elk was so badly bruised as to be of little value, but we obtained enough for our immediate use, which we carried to the camp. The next morning we skinned and cut up our elk, Blackwell securing the meat for his dog, and my brother took the skin. Soon after, Benjamin arrived with the man James Gamble, and the two dogs he had been sent to procure, in a sleigh, which gave the other men a conveyance in which they returned home. Gamble, Benjamin and myself started again for elk about one o'clock the same day. After reaching the top of the hill, we struck a northwestern course, and went about five miles when we encamped. The next morning before we had proceeded three quarters of a mile, we found where three large bucks had been feeding during the previous night. About a mile farther we discovered them lying down, and let loose two of the best dogs.

One of the elk came forward to meet the dogs, the other two started off to the south. The one which remained maintained his ground for a time, but the dogs were so furious that he finally started off in a westerly direction, ran eight miles, and stopped to fight the dogs. From appearances we judged that he must have remained here about half an hour. We traveled on as fast as possible in a direct westerly course toward Kettle Creek, for about ten miles from where the elk had stopped, when Gamble remarked that the elk would not stop in such open woods as we were then traversing, and that we had better encamp. I told him that it could not be more than two or three miles to Kettle Creek, and perhaps he would stop on a rock in going down the hill. Accordingly we went two miles farther where we found good camping ground, and as the others were tired and wanted to rest, I told them to build a fire while I continued on to see if I could learn any thing of the dogs. After running about a mile I came to a high bluff where I stood listening until I thought I heard them. I then ascended a tree which stood near, when I could distinctly hear the barking of the dogs, about two miles distant on the other side of the creek. I called to Benjamin and Gamble, and they hurried along in my track. When they had passed two or three rods by the tree in which I was concealed I set up a yell like the cry of a panther. They looked up the tree, and seeing a dark object in the branches, they were very much frightened. After enjoying their alarm a moment I laughed, and told them to hurry on and I would come down immediately. We went in the direction from which the sounds proceeded, crossed Kettle Creek on the ice, and found the elk on a rock fighting the dogs. The rock was about fifteen feet by thirty on the surface, and was fifteen feet above the creek on the side next the creek, and four feet on the other. We encamped within five rods of the rock, and prepared our supper. After some consultation, we concluded not to attempt catching the elk until daylight, as it was now two o'clock at night. We accordingly called off the dogs, and arranged it so as to take turns in watching him. I watched for the first two hours, when he lay down and I awoke Gamble, who was to take the next watch. In a short time he laid down again, thinking the elk would not leave the rock before morning. At daybreak I awoke and perceived that the elk had gone, and the dogs were asleep. I soon dressed and took the dogs to the rock and sent them after the elk, which had taken the back track. I thought that if the dogs found and attacked him he would return to the rock. When I returned to the camp I found the others dressing and told them what I had done. They thought we might as well pack up and start in pursuit immediately after breakfast, as they did not believe he would return to the rock. In a short time, he came bounding back, and again took his station on the rock. We found that we could not rope him while he remained on the rock, and we therefore withdrew and allowed him to come off. He went down to the creek, when I cut a large club and went on the rock, telling the others to drive the elk back. They let the dogs loose and he came toward the rock. As he passed me, I gave him a blow with the club, which made little impression on him, when I gave him two more with all my strength, which dropped him to his knees. He rose, wheeled around and went to the lower side of the rock, against which he backed himself, and stood warding off the attack of the dogs. I took a rope to that part of the rock which overhung the elk, and threw the rope over his horns, drawing it close down to his head. We then attached the other end of the rope to a tree, and proceeded to build around him a pen of logs, ten by twenty-two feet square, and twelve feet high. When it was completed, we threw in browse sufficient to supply him four or five days, and then laid poles across the top, which we covered with hemlock boughs, forming a snug and comfortable shelter. Before leaving him, we gave him about twenty feet of slack rope. We then packed up and started for home, encamping that night about five miles below, on the west side of the creek. The next morning, when we started, the snow was three feet deep. We crossed Kettle Creek, and struck a direct east course, expecting to reach a creek with which we were acquainted, but missed our way, and struck Cedar Creek, ten miles from where we had started in the morning. As it was becoming dark, we provided ourselves with torches of yellow pine, and started down the creek. After wading five miles through water from two to ten inches deep, we reached Big Pine Creek about two o'clock in the morning. We had now either to wade through the creek, then very high and full of slush ice, or to go around a mountain and reach the creek at a crossing place a mile and a half below. We finally determined to cross, if possible, where we were, as we were nearer home, and on the opposite shore lived

three lumbermen, who could afford us the refreshments we felt
we so much needed. I went out into the stream, to see
whether a crossing was practicable. The water was three
feet deep, unusually rapid, and a short distance below was
a deep hole, but I resolved to make the attempt. Returning to the shore I took hold of Benjamin with one hand,
while in the other I carried the axe; Benjamin took hold
of Gamble, who in his other hand carried a stick with which
to brace us against the force of the current. The bottom was
rocky, with moss growing upon it, which aided us in retaining
a footing. We finally succeed in reaching safely the other
shore, a distance of fifteen rods. Our dogs swam after us,
but the best one was carried down under the ice and drowned.
About four o'clock we reached the lumberman's, and they
immediately arose and prepared some refreshments, for us,
which we took, and without stopping to rest, we started
for my brother's, six miles distant. The traveling was so
difficult that we did not arrive there until two o'clock in the
afternoon. The next day, as I was quite lame, I hired four
men to go and bring the elk home. There was a kind of
trail to Kettle Creek fifteen miles, and from there to the
pen was ten miles. In the afternoon of the second day
they reached the place, but found that the elk had thrown
down the pen, gnawed off the rope, and escaped with twenty
feet of it. The party returned, and gave me an account of
my misfortune. I was still lame, and hired three others
to catch him. They were to have sixty dollars when they
had secured him uninjured, and assisted me to bring him
home. They started out with two good dogs, and had
not gone more than three miles before they found him entangled by the rope among the trees and bushes. They secured him, built a pen around him, and leaving with him a
supply of food, came and informed me of their success. I
hired another man and proceeded to the spot. In four
days we brought him in — a large and beautiful animal,
with antlers five and a half feet long.

CHAPTER IX.

ELK HUNTING ON THE SUSQUEHANNA.

WHEN I lived on Kenzua Flats, in 1816, I went to see Cornplanter, about catching some elk. He said that I could not do it; that no Indian of the Six Nations had done it, or any white man that he knew of. He said that young elk three or four months old had been caught, but no live, full-grown one could be — they were lords of the forest. I told him that I had caught or assisted in catching and leading in three. He asked how we led them, and I informed him. He said he did not know but it was possible, but he did not believe I could take one that winter on the Allegany, as he thought they were larger and wilder than those on the Susquehannah. I told him that if he would show me the track of an elk — I did not care how large — the larger the better; I would willingly wager a small sum of money that I would bring one in alive. He said that he could show plenty of elk-tracks. I told him to find a man that I could hire, and I would employ him. He brought a man who charged a dollar a day, which I agreed to pay him on condition that he would find a track. He said there was no doubt but that we could find one. There was no rope to be procured except one that belonged to Cornplanter, for which he wanted two dollars, but agreed to refund the money if I returned the rope uninjured. I agreed to his terms, and left the money. As we parted he wanted to shake hands, saying that he never expected to see me again if I attempted to catch an elk alive. The next morning the Indian I had engaged joined me, and I entered into a partnership with a Mr. Campbell, each of us to stand half the expense and have half the profits. We hired two other men who were to have all they killed and half that we killed. On the third day of January, Campbell and myself, the two white men, the Indian, and four dogs started up Kenzua Creek. We went about twelve miles up the south branch, and encamped for the night. The next morning we continued about six miles, to the top of a hill, and halted. The Indian said we would find elk within four or five miles of this spot. I proposed to divide, Campbell, myself and the Indian each taking a separate course while the two others should remain to build a camp where we would all meet at night. Accordingly, as soon as we had eaten dinner we all started, and remained out until dark, when we met at the camp. No one had discovered any indications of elk. The next morning I told them we would hunt one day more, each upon a different course. I took a direct easterly course, and the others chose each his own route. At night all but the Indian came in, without having discovered any signs of an elk. I told Campbell I thought it useless to hunt here longer. as there were probably no elk in the vicinity. About eight o'clock one of the party discovered the Indian coming in, followed apparently by one of the dogs. He remarked that one of the dogs was loose, and following the Indian in. I found the dogs all in their places, and told the men I thought it was a wolf they saw. At this moment he stopped and we saw at a glance that it was a panther. We sprang forward with our guns, when he turned and moved off. We followed him two miles, without obtaining a shot at him, when we returned to the camp. We paid the Indian and let him go. I told Campbell I would not be disappointed in this manner, but would hunt all winter rather than give up. We concluded to go to the headwaters of the Susquehannah, and accordingly started on the eighth of January, going about fifteen miles up the Kenzua, and encamped for the night. The next day, when we had proceeded about twelve miles we arrived at a place where a village now stands, but at that time there was but a solitary house in which lived a family named Smith. The man had gone to procure a barrel of flour, and since his departure a deep snow had fallen. He had now been gone three days beyond the expected time, and the supply of provisions and fuel which he had left was nearly exhausted. In addition to the prospect of starvation which stared them in the face, his family were harrassed with the fear that he had perished in the snow. The next day we prepared her a supply of fire-wood, left a loaf of bread and flour enough to supply her for two days, and promised to send a man back, on our arrival at the canoe place. We arrived there a little before night, and engaged a man named Burt to go back to the distressed family. He took with him some corn meal and potatoes, and we continued on to Isaac Lyman's, about twelve miles farther. He asked us to come in; we got to talking about elk-hunting, and I asked him what a full-grown live elk would be worth. He said from three to four hundred dollars. I asked him if he would purchase one if I had the luck to catch one. He replied that he had not the means, but would like to join us, and would furnish three men, a horse, and all the provisions necessary, and have one-half the profits. After some consultation, Campbell and I finally consented to accept the proposal. The whole party, consisting of Campbell, myself, three assistants, a horse and four dogs, started the next morning, taking the road to the Susquehannah River. About twelve miles from Lyman's we came upon the track of eight elk, going west. We followed about four miles and encamped for the night. The next morning Campbell, myself, and one of the men continued on the track of the elk, leaving the others to build a shanty. We went about five miles, started the elk and killed one, with which we returned to the camp. We sent one of the men home with the meat, and started with the other two for the Susquehannah. The man who went home was to return to the camp in three days, with a supply of provisions. After traveling seven or eight miles, we came to where a large drove of elk had been some time before. We hunted during the day to ascertain what course they had taken, and about five miles distant we came to where they had lain the preceding night. Campbell and one of the men George Ayres, went forward, while the other man and myself remained behind with the dogs. They were to call to us when they saw the elk, and we were to let the dogs loose, though I told him I did not believe there were any there we would want to catch, as I thought they were all fawns and does. After they had gone a short distance they saw them, and counted forty-two. They called to us, and we let the dogs loose. The elk scattered, and each of the dogs took after a separate animal, but none of them stopped, and we did not kill any. The dogs all came back that night, and the next morning we went so[u]theast, and found signs of elk, but they all appeared to be small ones. By this time Mr. Lyman's hands wished to go home, so we told them we would keep on to the southeast, and they might go. The following morning they said they did not like to go, as the tracks might be filled with snow. We then said we would strike

the road and they might go home from there, while we
would go to our log hut, and procure some more provisions.
When we reached the road, we told them they might as well
go to the shanty and stay with us that night, as it was late.
We found two men there with an abundance of provisions.
The next morning two men left, while Ayres and another
remained. We hunted the next three days without seeing
any tracks which we thought best to follow. We then came
back to the road, and the remaining two men left for home
with two dogs. We sent word by them to Lyman to send
provisions to the camp on Kettle Creek, where we should be
in a few days. We hunted the next two days without accomplishing any thing, when we returned to the camp. On
our arrival there I told Campbell he might take his choice
to make a fire or kill some game. He preferred to kill the
game, and I proceeded to cut wood and make a fire. He
had not been gone more than half an hour when I heard the
report of his gun. He soon came in, dragging a large fat
deer, which enabled us to make an excellent supper. After
we had eaten, we began to talk about our success, when
Campbell said he would hunt but three days longer unless
we were more successful. I told him I should hunt until the
snow went off before I would give up. The next morning
we went south toward Sinemahoning, seeing no signs of
elk, and at night we returned to our camp. The following
day Campbell was somewhat unwell, and I told him if he
would remain and keep camp and dry some of the venison,
I would go out toward Pine Creek, to which he consented.
After proceeding about seven miles, I found where an elk
had been browsing. The manner in which the limbs had
been pulled down showed that it must have been a very
large animal. I hunted in the vicinity several hours to ascertain the direction in which he went, but the tracks were
so old that I could not decide. As I arrived at the camp a
man came along who said that he had seen in the road the
largest elk tracks he ever saw. I told Campbell of the indications I had discovered, and that the tracks were probably those of the same animal. We invited the man to
eat supper with us, as we were greatly obliged to him for
the information he had given us. Campbell thought we
could not catch him, as we had not sufficient force. I told
him I could take the elk alone. The next morning we started at daybreak, and found the tracks of the elk, going west.
A mile and a half farther he had lain the previous night.

In a moment Campbell saw him, and cried out, " There he stands: the largest elk I ever saw! " I let the dogs go, they attacked him vigorously, and he ran south ten miles to Kettle Creek. He then ran around a hill, and turned up the east branch which he ascended four miles on the ice when he broke through, into water about four feet deep. Here the dogs worried him, as we judged, about two hours, when he started again, ran up a hill, and halted on a rock. The dogs pursued him to the rock, and then returned to us. We met them two or three miles from the elk, which had taken a circuitous course, so that the track at one place was but a fourth of a mile from the rock on which he was stationed, while it was two miles to follow the track. The dogs tried to go directly to the elk, but we thought they saw something else, and compelled them to keep the track, reaching the elk about dark. Campbell made ready the rope, while I cut a pole about fifteen feet long. He went to the south side of the rock with the dogs, to call his attention in that direction, while I mounted the rock on the north side, and endeavored to put the rope over his horns with the pole. He wheeled and came toward me, when I jumped from the rock, and he turned again to the dogs. About eight feet from the rock stood a hemlock tree, about two feet in diameter, with branches six or eight feet above the ground. It occurred to me that if I could climb this it would be an easy matter to slip the noose over the horns of the elk. I made the attempt, but did not succeed as my moccasins were frozen. I pulled them off and tried again, but with no better success. I then took off my coat, which was by no means pleasant, as the weather was intensely cold, but it enabled me to climb the tree. Campbell then passed the pole and rope up to me, and called off the dogs. I shouted, and the elk turned and advanced toward me, when I slipped the noose over his horns, and with a jerk drew it tight. I then descended and attached the end of the rope to a tree about forty feet from the elk, and we pulled him from the rock, when we left him for the night. It was then half-past eleven, and we were compelled to go three-quarters of a mile to find a suitable place for encamping. Arriving there I was attacked so severely with nervous headache that I could scarcely walk. Campbell, in looking for a suitable camping-place, found a shanty which had been built by a party of hunters the previous night. We found here a bed of coals and plenty of wood cut. Campbell replenished the fire, and prepared a decoction of hemlock boughs, which greatly relieved me. He then cooked supper, and when we had eaten, it was two o'clock. Our next thought was to procure assistance enough to convey home our elk. The nearest settlement was forty miles distant, and I told Campbell that as I was the stronger I had better go. He said he preferred going himself, as he did not understand how to take care of an elk. As he desired it I consented. He started the next morning, taking with him the dogs, went to Cowdersport, the nearest settlement, and in 4 days returned with three men and a horse.

About ten o'clock one night during his absence I heard bells on the east side of Kettle Creek. I walked down to the creek, and as I reached the bank a sleigh drawn by two horses drove into the creek on the opposite side. The weight of the horses broke the ice the entire width of the stream, and when they reached the bank they could not draw the sleigh out of the water. The man then went to the hind end of the sleigh with a bar of iron, which he used as a lever, and spoke to the horses. They made another attempt to extricate the sleigh, and fell. He came to the forward end, and for the first time saw me. He was startled at the unexpected appearance of a human form in that wilderness, and cried out, " In the name of God, what are you? A man; or a ghost? " I assured him that I was flesh and blood, and he said I should have spoken to him. I replied I was so intent in watching his operations that I had not thought of speaking. He asked me to start the horses, while he went behind and pushed with his lever. I told him it was useless; the horses had already tried, and were unable to draw the sleigh out. He went in, however, and spoke to the horses, when they made another effort and fell again. I told him to come out of the water and go to the camp, and I would be there soon with his horses and sleigh. He was quite willing to accept my offer, and started for the camp. I detached the horses from the sleigh, brought them to the top of the bank and connected them by a chain which I found in the sleigh to the end of the tongue. As they could now obtain firm footing, they brought the sleigh to the top of the bank without difficulty. Just as I was starting for the camp, another man arrived at the opposite bank, with a horse and cutter, and wished to cross. I advised him to leave his cutter and ride his horse through the creek, which he did, and we went to the camp together. On our arrival there we found the other man in excruciating pain. His clothes were so frozen before he reached the camp, that he could scarcely walk, and he had nearly perished. They both believed that they would have frozen, had it not been for the assistance I rendered. The following morning as they did not like to leave me there alone, I accompanied them to their destination, ten miles distant, where we left the sleighs and harness, and rode the horses back to the camp. Quite early the next morning Campbell arrived with the four men, the horses and sleigh. We immediately set to removing the elk, and in two days we arrived with him at Cowdersport. We there settled with Lyman, he to be one-half owner of the elk, and Campbell and myself, each a quarter. Lyman sold one-half his share to a man named Waterman, for two hundred and fifty dollars, the elk being valued at a thousand dollars. We all four went with him to Olean, forty miles distant, where we obtained twelve dollars by exhibiting him. We then exhibited him at a place six miles farther, and made six dollars more. At the latter place a man bet five dollars that he could hold him by grasping his nose with one hand, with his other arm around his horns. He lost the money, however, the animal striking him in the back with one of its hind feet, so severely that it drew blood.

December tenth, 1818, I started out on an elk-catching expedition, accompanied by John Campbell, Joseph Darling, and an Indian named Billy Fox. The first day, Campbell killed a fine, fat deer, and in the evening, at a distance of seven miles from home, we regaled ourselves with a steak from it. The following day we dismissed Darling, and sent Fox to hunt for an elk-track, while Campbell and I dried meat. Fox crossed Kenzua Creek, and went in the direction of Stump Creek, where he found a track. He ascertained its direction, and returned to the camp. The next morning, as there was bright moonlight, we started at three o'clock. We followed the track but a short distance, as it was an old one. We ascended a hill, and found the track of an elk which had passed that morning. After following the track three-quarters of a mile, we saw the elk feeding upon moss. We let loose our three dogs, two of which chased him to a rock, while the other one turned and came back to us in a short time, and the two, after stopping the elk, went to the camp. When we reached the rock the elk had gone, but we had one good dog, which soon sent him bounding back. We stood

[59]

aside and let him mount the rock, but when we attempted
to rope him he leaped from the rock at a place where it
was ten feet to the ground and ran down the hill. It was
nearly dark, but notwithstanding, we chased him about two
miles, when the dogs stopped him on another rock. In an
hour we had secured him. I then sent for men and a horse
to assist us in conveying him home, which was forty miles
distant. We arrived there in three days, and Campbell sold
his share for two hundred dollars. I soon after sold my share
for two hundred and sixty dollars, with the privilege of exhibiting him in Warren, which brought me fourteen dollars
and a half. This elk was captured with less trouble, expense and time than any I ever caught.

A few days after, Morrison, Campbell and myself departed
from Warren on another elk-hunt. At Kenzua we hired a
man, two horses and four good dogs. We went to an old
camp, about sixteen miles distant, and sent back the man
and team. The next morning we started, and after traveling twelve miles we struck the tracks of two elk, which
we followed till we found them quite fresh, when, it being
late, we encamped. The day following, a warm south
wind was blowing, accompanied by a drizzling rain, started
out, and when we had gone two miles we found where they
had rested during the night. Letting the dogs go, they
chased them twenty miles, when one of the elk halted upon
a rock. We arrived there about dark, and in half an hour
succeeded in capturing him. We then built a fire by the
side of a projecting rock, and my companions went to
sleep notwithstanding the rain and mud, but I sat up and
kept fire, as I could not sleep. In the morning the rain
ceased, but as we all felt the need of some repose, we concluded to remain there another day. We were now thirty
miles from the head of Stump Creek, thirty miles from Kenzua. For that place Campbell and Morrison started the
next day, to procure a horse, as the easiest manner of removing
an elk was to lead it with a horse. After going fifteen miles
Campbell returned, saying that he did not wish to walk so
far, when Morrison could do the business as well without
him. At the end of three days Morrison returned with a
man and a horse. In the meantime Campbell and I had
cut a road through the underbrush twelve miles. With our
increased force we started for Kenzua, arriving there in 2 days.

We had contracted with a Mr. Tanner, of Warren to take
the elk at five hundred dollars, if it was a large, handsome

one, but as the one we had did not answer the conditions, we sent word to him that he might take the elk at a lower price, or we would take him east, where we would undoubtedly find a good sale for him. Tanner said that if we would take the animal to Warren, he would purchase it at some price. We accordingly built a raft upon which we conveyed it to Warren. When Tanner saw it he offered three hundred dollars, if one of us would assist him in taking it to Pittsburgh, and to the one who went he would pay a dollar a day. We accepted the terms, and I offered sixteen dollars to either of the others who would go and leave me at liberty to return to my family. Morrison and Campbell each offered me sixteen dollars if I would go, as they thought I could manage the elk better than either of them; and Tanner offered me all I could make by exhibiting him until we arrived within forty-five miles of Pittsburgh. I concluded to accept the offer and set to building [a] cabin on a raft, for the elk. We took him on board with the assistance of a horse, and the next day started for Pittsburgh.

In 1822, Campbell and myself hired another man named Avery, and went out about twenty miles for an elk-hunt. Having established our camp, Campbell and myself left the next day, leaving Avery to keep camp. For three days we hunted without any success, and returned to the camp. During our absence Avery had been kept in a constant state of alarm by wild animals. Two panthers and eight wolves had prowled around the camp, and so terrified him that he declared he would not again stay alone in the woods for all the elk in them. We wanted him to remain until we had taken an elk, which he agreed to do, if he could be with us while we hunted. We accordingly took him with us the next day, but when we returned to our camp at night, he was nearly exhausted, having waded through deep snow all day, and the following day was quite willing to remain in the camp. At a moment when Avery was out for wood, Campbell and I packed provisions sufficient for three days, and when we left the camp, he supposed we would return at night. For two days we hunted without finding a track that we considered best to follow, and on the morning of the third started for the camp, but soon struck the track of a large elk, which had just passed and was within a short distance. We let loose the dogs and gave chase. The snow was two and a half feet deep, with a stiff crust, rendering it extremely difficult for the elk to run, while the dogs could

skip along over the crust, and worry him at every step. He
ran toward our camp seven miles, when he turned and stood
at bay upon a large rock. We roped him without much
difficulty, and watched him that night. The next morning
we started for the camp, arriving there about eleven o'clock,
and found Avery with a sad tale. He said that after our
departure the wolves kept howling around the camp, and as
night began to approach, an examination into the stores re-
vealed the cruel trick we had played upon him. When the
suspicion flashed upon his mind that he was doomed to pass
another night here, with no company, save that of the wolves
and panthers, which might possibly form a repast of him
before morning, he gave vent to his feelings in a flood of
tears. The next day he resolved to leave the camp, and go
home, but before he had proceeded more than a mile, he
heard the howling of wolves, and as he had no gun, he hastened back to the camp. He had a good knife, an axe and
a tomahawk, and to these means of defence he added clubs
and pointed sticks. He also kept a large fire constantly
blazing, and built a scaffold about five feet high, on which
he slept. He had passed the time, notwithstanding all these
precautions, in constant anxiety, and was heartily glad to
see human faces again, but when he learned that we had
captured an elk, he was much more delighted. We all went
to a traveled road about fifteen miles distant, and from there
sent Avery to procure a man and horse, to assist in taking
the elk home, while Campbell and I returned to the camp.
On the second day after leaving us, he returned with a Mr.
Dixon and a horse. We started the next morning for our
elk, but when we arrived at the place where we had left
him, he was not there. He, as one had done several years
before, probably commenced licking the rope and continued
until it was chewed off, and escaped. We let the dogs loose,
and followed ourselves about two miles, where the elk stopped
among some logs. Now that we had him we resolved to
make sure of him, so we watched him all night, and the
next day took him to the camp. From there we traveled
by way of Kenzua, and in three days arrived at my residence
near Cold Spring, in Catarraugus county, New York. We
remained there a few days, and exhibited the animal, and
then went with him to Ellicottville, where we sold him for
one hundred and ten dollars. This was the last elk I ever
caught, the low price obtained for him making the business
so unprofitable that I abandoned it entirely.

CHAPTER X.

ELK-HUNTING (CONTINUED)

IN 1800, a party of four, my brother Jacob, George Wilson, Joshua Knapp, and myself proceeded on an elk-hunt. Expecting the campaign would last about six weeks, we took an abundant supply of provisions, consisting of flour, potatoes, sugar, chocolate, corn, and a quantity of salt with which to cure our meat. We were also provided with half a dozen empty barrels for the meat, an iron pot holding about six gallons, a camp kettle, four axes, a broad axe, a chalk line, a canoe howel, (an instrument for scooping out canoes,) a drawing knife, two augurs, six tomahawks, and several pounds of powder and lead. Each of us took, besides, a rifle, two knives, a quart cup, four shirts and two blankets, not forgetting a supply of soap. Thus equipped, and accompanied by four dogs, we set out, placing our effects in a canoe, which two of the party pushed up the stream, while the others hunted along the shore. We left on the 12th of October, starting for the Big Meadows. The second day we saw seven elk, in the river, eating moss. As Knapp said he had never killed an elk, I told him to take two of the dogs and go. As the dogs started for the elk, two does turned, advanced toward them, but as they met, the does left the water ran down the stream about half a mile, and went into the creek where Wilson and my brother happened to be with the canoe. The does stopped in the water, where it was three feet deep, and they shot them, dragged them out of the water, and cut their throats. I then sent my dogs after an elk, which ran into the stream from the east bank, near where they were pulling the canoe over some rapids. The elk approached within thirty feet of them before they were observed, but they were so much excited that they did not take good aim, and both missed. The elk ran down the stream, about half a mile, when the dogs stopped them, and Knapp shot one of them. Two of us skinned and dressed the elk, while the other two made a pine trough holding about four barrels, in which to salt the meat. When the meat was cut from the bone and nicely salted down in the trough, we put it under a bank in a cool place, and covered it over with large, flat stones, over which we placed larger ones, and then rolled on two large logs which we fastened down with withes. We then broke the bones and extracted the marrow, of which, and the fat, we secured forty-five pounds from the three elk. The next day, leaving the meat there, but taking the tallow and skins, we proceeded up the creek, and the second day killed two large, fat does, which we dressed and quartered, and laid the meat in the canoe. We arrived at the place of rendezvous about two o'clock, and proceeded to erect a log house. When this was completed, we tried the tallow, salted our meat, and in two days set out with provisions sufficient for a couple of weeks. Jacob and Wilson ascended the creek to the Big Elk Lick. When they arrived there they counted forty-seven elk in the vicinity. They tied up their dogs in blankets, so that they could not see, hear, or make any noise, and shot eight elk, singling out the largest and fattest. When the first ones fell, the whole herd commenced squealing, creating such a noise as to make the ground tremble. The men had but about a bushel of salt with them, and drove away the rest of the elk, not wishing to destroy wantonly more than they could save. Wilson was inexperienced in elk-hunting, and was alarmed. He said that the elk would strike the wounded one, run their horns against the trees, and jump to a great height, some of them touching branches fifteen feet high. On the day they started for the licks Knapp and myself went up the Marsh Fork about five miles, and came upon the track of seven elk, which we followed into the marsh and there encamped. The marsh contained about two thousand acres and was surrounded by bluff hills. In high water it was overflowed, but was dry in summer. In the morning I ascended one of the bluffs, where I could see the whole of the marsh, and discovered the elk about half a mile off. After observing them awhile I descended, ate breakfast, and we started out after the elk. I went forward, telling Knapp to keep his dog back. As we approached the elk they sprang to their feet and ran off. We let the dogs loose, each taking after different elk. He followed his dog and I followed mine. In a short time I heard the report of his gun, but followed on after my elk for about seven miles, when I returned to the place where I had left my companion. I asked him where was the elk that I had heard him shoot. He replied that as he fired the elk fell, and he supposed him dead. Laying down his gun and bag of flour, he approached the elk, placed his foot upon his antlers, and attempted to cut his throat, but as soon as the knife touched his neck the elk sprang up, and seeing the bag of flour, he rushed at it, struck his antlers through it and ran off with the flour above his head. We started in pursuit, and followed the track to a dry, stony ridge, where we could no longer distinguish it, and we struck across to our camp, arriving there a little after dark. As we had bread enough for only two days, we concluded to go down to the block-house and recruit. The others had been there before us, and left word upon a shingle that they had killed eight elk, and there was still a chance to kill more. They desired us to come up with the canoe after the meat, which Knapp wished to do; but I resolved not to join the others and incur their ridicule until I had met with better success. Knapp said he should take the canoe and meet the others, even if he was compelled to go alone. I accordingly put up a supply of provisions and prepared to hunt alone. Just before I started, however, Knapp's courage failed, and he concluded to accompany me. We proceeded up Big Pine Creek, in the direction the others had taken. When we had gone about three miles we discovered five elk in the creek eating moss. I asked Knapp for his gun, so that I could fire twice without loading. He handed it to me, and remained behind, holding back his dog, while I crept along to within sixty yards of them, with my dog behind me. As one of them raised his head I fired, and the elk fell. The others gathered around it, and I snatched up Knapp's gun and shot another. The three others then left the water and started up the hill. I let my dog go, and he singled out a large buck, which he stopped about a mile and a half ahead. I tried to drive him back to the creek by throwing clubs, but he would not go. I shot him low in the breast, so as to wound without killing him. This started him toward the water, and when he reached it Knapp shot him. We then brought up our canoes, which were two and a half miles below, skinned the elk, put them into the canoe, and proceeded with them to the block-house. Expecting the other party down the next day, we left word on a shingle that we had killed ten elk, and then left the camp to hunt in the vicinity. We went down the creek and returned about three o'clock. The others were there, and as we approached the cabin we heard them say they wished they had killed a few more, so as to have at least one more than we. On going into the cabin they asked us where our other seven elk were, as they saw but three. We replied that we left them at the Big Marsh. They said it would be a difficult job to bring them down, in which opinion we fully concurred in our own minds, especially as the principal part of the difficulty consisted in killing them. They sat in silence until we told them that the elk we left at the Big Marsh were still alive and at liberty, which piece of intelligence raised their spirits greatly. When I informed them of Knapp's adventure, they nearly went wild with merriment, lying on the floor and rolling in an ecstacy of mirth. When their merriment had subsided, it was judged that Knapp should be randeled, inasmuch as he had transgressed an important rule of the chase. The rule was that when a gun was discharged it should instantly be reloaded, so that the hunter would be prepared for any exigency; but Knapp had lain down his gun empty, instead of reloading it, and thus lost the game. The operation of randeling was the usual punishment among hunters for any neglect of duty, and consisted in seating the offender upon a stool, while others, in turn went up and pulled his hair, sometimes plucking out a few. The odor of this adventure never left Knapp.

The following morning we took the canoe and all our tools, and ascended to the Lick, where we intended to make another canoe. No elk had been there since Jacob and Wilson had made such havoc among them. The next day we concluded to start out, each one in a different direction, and to meet again at night. Jacob tossed up with Wilson, and Knapp with me, to decide which should take the west side of the creek, that side being preferable. It fell on Wilson and me to take the west side. I went down the creek to where a branch came in and found there some old elk tracks, which I followed until it was so late that I could not return to the camp that night. I encamped on the elk-track, and spent the most dismal night that I ever experienced. The wolves flocked around me in droves, and their unearthly howling, mingled with the dismal screeching of the owls overhead made a concert of sounds that banished sleep from my eyes the greater part of the night. I sat in my shanty, with my gun in one hand, a tomahawk in the other, and a knife by my side. When the wolves became unusually uproarous, I would send the dog out to drive them away, and if they drove him in, I would fire in among them. At length, toward morning, I fell asleep from sheer exhaustion, and slept until daylight, when I arose, ate my breakfast, and started again on the elk-track. About four miles from where I had slept I arrived at a creek running southwest and emptying into Pine Creek at a point about five miles below the Lick. The elk had ascended the creek, and thinking it would not be best to follow I descended the stream to its junction with Pine Creek. When I arrived at the mouth I found the others there making a canoe, and the sight of a human countenance was a welcome one to me, with the horrors of the previous night still fresh in my mind. As I approached them I concealed myself and imitated the howl of a wolf. After the lessons of the previous night, I made a very successful imitation, and thought I would try my powers by imitating the cry of a panther. I repeated the cry twice, when they all stood listening in considerable consternation, and one of them cried out, "It is a panther!" My brother's practiced ear, however, detected the fraud, and he replied that he thought it was a two-legged one, and would soon make his appearance. As I came up, they asked what luck, expecting I had killed something. I marked three, and they asked, why I had killed three elk up there. I told them to give themselves no uneasiness about my elk, as they were as well able to take care of themselves as ever. The rest of the party had killed nothing. In about a week we had finished three good canoes, each capable of carrying from twenty-five to fifty hundred weight. We started on another hunt, examining the country throughout, but could find no elk. We then commenced hunting deer. Three men stationed themselves on the creek, about a mile apart, while the other, with the dogs, scoured the woods. When he saw a deer, he let a dog go, which would chase it to the creek, and as it ran up or down the stream. would come within shot of one of the men. If the man saw another deer, he let loose another dog, and in this manner we frequently killed three or four deer in a day. In five days we killed fifteen handsome animals, one being driven in by a wolf. We secured the skins, tallow, and meat, and as the water was so low that we could not get over the rapids with our canoe, we continued to hunt. In three days we killed five more, when a rain caused a rise in the water, which enabled us to start down with our canoes, loaded with our tools and game. In five days we arrived at my father's residence, where we divided our skins, venison, and tallow, giving to Wilson and Knapp a few more than an even proportion of the skins, as they had furnished a greater share of the supplies. They also took the two large canoes, and we the small one, and a rifle worth thirty dollars.

After our return that winter, we were very successful in hunting, my brother and myself killing forty-seven deer, fifteen bears and two elk.

CHAPTER XI.

THE elk is a member of the same family as the deer, but is a much more noble specimen than the common deer, growing sometimes sixteen hands high, which is the height of a medium sized horse, and often weighing six hundred pounds. The buck is provided with large and beautiful antlers. These grow the second year to the length of two or two and a half feet, being sometimes a single spike, but often with one or two branches. The sixth year the antlers are from five to six and a half feet long, with several branches, the largest number I ever observed being seven on one antler and six on the other; the two which projected forward being from fifteen to eighteen inches long. Between the nostril and the eye is an opening or vent through which they blow to produce the peculiar noise which is heard during the rutting season, or when they are frightened. This noise in a doe resembles very nearly in tone the whinny of a horse, while that produced by the buck is not as shrill, being somewhat more like the braying of an ass, but can be heard sometimes at a distance of three miles. During the rutting season this sound often betrays the elk to the hunter. He can easily perceive whether it proceeds from a buck or a doe, and replies to it in the tone of the opposite sex, until the animal approaches within shot. In the month of March the elk sheds his antlers, and new ones begin to grow about the middle of April, which arrive at their full growth in August. During the process of their formation they are covered with a substance of a reddish-brown color, called the velvet under which course innumerable blood-vessels. At this period they are extremely sensitive, but about the middle of August, when they have attained their full growth, they lose their sense of feeling, and the animal begins to rub them against the trees to remove the velvet. During this process the antlers have a gory appearance, but at length the extraneous matter is all removed, and they appear in their prefect state, seamed in every direction by the traces of the blood vessels with which they were covered during their growth. The tail of the elk is about five inches long, and is similar to that of a bear. Their color in winter is a dun, which changes in April or May to a light reddish brown, except the hips, which are always yellow, like those of a deer. The motion of the elk is an ambling trot, which it will maintain for a long period, without apparent fatigue. Sometimes they will run six or seven days before they become exhausted. In their manner of breeding as well as many other things, they resemble domestic cattle. They bring forth their young in May — rarely more than one at a time, and never more than two.

The most favorable time for hunting elk is in the month of August, when they herd together, and the bucks are very fat. I have sometimes seen as many as sixty in one herd. At this season they utter a peculiar hollow roar, which can be heard at a great distance, and are constantly fighting with each other. The hunter approached them cautiously with dogs, and when near enough he let the dogs loose, and the elk, instead of running, would face the dogs. The hunter now crept nearer, and shot them, keeping himself concealed. They would gather around their fallen companions, making a great noise, which with the barking of the dogs, made it appear as if the forest was full of them. In this manner I have fired eight times, killing five, without being discovered. Not wishing to continue the slaughter, I then came out and shouted at them, and even then they did not start, but stood as if spell-bound. At length the whole herd turned and trotted off. At this season they collect together in great numbers at the elk-licks, where they remain a week or two. In one instance they assembled in such numbers at a lick that the trees for an acre or two around were killed by the friction of their horns in rubbing off the velvet, and thus destroying the bark. When they met near the licks they would fight so that the weaker ones could not reach the lick in three or four days. From June to the middle of August they went to the rivers to eat moss, remaining a short time, and then return to the woods and scatter themselves until the first of November. The does and fawns would collect in droves and remain together until the last of March, when they would again scatter through the woods. About the tenth of June the does would leave their young at a little distance, and come to the river for the moss in its bed, and the tender feed which grew on the banks. If we saw a doe near the river without her fawn, we started after her with our best dogs, and she would run at once to where she had left her fawn, with which she would take to the water. When the dogs pressed her hard, she would turn and face them, to protect her fawn, until she had reached a place where the water was deep enough to protect them from the dogs. If we wished to secure the fawn we shot the doe, and then sent the dogs into the water, plunging in after them ourselves, to prevent them from destroying the fawn. This was the most successful manner of taking young elk. On taking them home we generally put them in a yard with a calf, to which it would become much attached. They were as easily trained to work as a colt or a steer. I have taken full grown buck elk which were very unmanageable at first, but after shedding their antlers they became tractable and were easily broken to the harness, and were ever after very gentle, except a short time in September and October, when their antlers were full-grown. A female elk will stand and suffer herself to be milked, and their milk is nearly equal to that of a cow, both in quality and quantity. In my opinion the elk would prove a valuable addition to our stock of domestic animals, if introduced among them. It possesses strength and speed superior to any other cloven-footed animal, while for food or milk they are equally valuable. Their growth is very rapid, and they are easily kept in good condition. Indeed, all the qualities which render the reindeer so indispensable to the inhabitants of Lapland, are possessed by the elk. When domesticated, they become greatly attached to the locality in which they were reared, and the animals with which they have associated. A doe which had been reared by our family with a cow, was taken twenty-four miles from home to stay with another tame elk. After staying there a month, the fence being left down it escaped and started for home, leaving an animal of its own species for those with which it had been accustomed to associate. It was ten days in coming home, stopping in every corn-field until driven out by the dogs. The men seeing it was a tame one did not molest it, and it arrived home in safety. When it met the cow which was its foster-mother, it manifested the greatest joy, and ever after kept near her, jealously driving away any other animal that approached.

When the first snow of winter comes, the elk paws it away and feeds upon the grass and herbage under it. When the snow becomes deep and crusted so that they cannot get

[71]

at the grass, they browse upon a small tree called elk-wood. This tree or shrub never grows more than five inches in diameter, and generally not as large. It has a scraggy top, and is easily reached and pulled down by the elk. This shrub must not be confounded with the one sometimes called moose-wood, which has a very tough, fibrous bark, and the proper name of which is leather-wood. When the elk-wood is scarce, they eat the twigs of basswood, elm, hickory or white ash. In severe storms they seek sheltered places, under rocks, the points of hills, or in hemlock thickets. A favorite resort for them is in places where old trees have been blown down, and a thick second growth of underbrush has sprung up. In the spring they scatter through the woods, alone or in pairs, seeking the heads of small streams, and other localities where the young feed first begins to start. Before the axe of the settler had leveled the forests in which they ranged, their most frequented resorts in the interior of Pennsylvania were between the Allegany and the Susquehannah, and on the west side of the north branch of the Susquehannah, from the Loyalsock Creek to the New York state line. I have found them most numerous in the western part of Lycoming and the eastern part of McKean counties, on the head waters of the Susquehannah and the Allegany.

The elk is the lord of the forest in which he ranges, no animal inhabiting the same localities being able to conquer him. Terrific combats sometimes ensue among themselves, and I have often found them dead in the woods, with deep wounds made by the antlers of their antagonists.

CHAPTER XII.

ELK AND BEAR HUNTING IN WINTER.

IN hunting elk in the winter, if the ice was strong enough, we would go up the creek in sleighs; but if it was too weak for that purpose we would take a hand-sleigh to carry our necessaries. It was usual for two or three of the party to go together; one staying along the river and watching, while the others went in search of tracks, and when they found one, followed it, and alarming the elk, it would generally make for the rocks on the bank of the creek, where, being stopped by the dogs, we could shoot them. Sometimes, after they had received a shot, they would fall fifty or sixty feet down the bank to the creek or towards it. When we shot them some distance from the creek, we took out their entrails, and sprinkled powder or sulphur around, to keep off the wild animals, and left the elk there with its skin on, until we could procure a horse to draw it to the river.

Bear-meat, at that time, brought a much higher price than elk-meat; bear oil and bear-skins were also in great demand. The skins sold for from four to ten dollars. If we saw a bear track when we were in pursuit of elk, we would always leave the elk and follow the bear. From the middle of January until July we did not make a business of hunting bears or elk. In our winter hunts we used to go to the Round Islands, and be gone from three to six days, killing, in that time, from six to eight elk. Sometimes we would kill three or four bears in one hunt. We seldom failed in killing a bear after having found the track. The dogs would either drive them up a tree or stop them. We owned three well-trained dogs. If we put them on a track they would not leave it for any other; they would always come when we called, and never go until we gave the word. Whenever a bear crossed the creek, the dogs always followed; if the water was too deep for us to wade through, we had to construct a float on which to cross, always keeping up the pursuit with suc-

cess. If the guns missed fire the dogs would manage to stop
the bear; they would not give up the chase unsuccessfully.
I have known them to tree a bear and remain by it two days.
During the three years that we lived at that place we never
lost one after we came up with it. The one that killed the
first of any kind of animal was to have the skin.

My brother killed from twenty-five to thirty elk and
twenty to twenty-five bears each year. I did not kill as
many. I usually killed from ten to twenty bears, and one
season I killed thirty-five elk. By fire-hunting, hunting in
the woods, and by hounding deer, my brother has taken as
many as seventy in a season. When the deer were fat, which
was about the last of October, we depended a great deal on
hounding them. About break of day we would send a dog
out after a deer; when he found one he would drive it towards
the creek where some of us were stationed to shoot it. If the
deer happened to cross the creek without our getting a shot,
we let another dog after it on the other side, to drive it to
the creek again. If a second deer came in sight during the
chase we let another go after it; and in this manner we have
had all the dogs out at once. Sometimes a dog would drive
one deer to the creek, and sometimes he would bring in two,
a doe and her fawn, or a doe and a buck. The three dogs
have, in this manner, in one chase, brought in five deer. In
that locality, I killed in one season, from the time we first
began to fire-hunt, in June, until the middle of January,
forty-seven deer. During one season, my brother killed, of
bears, elk and deer, nearly two hundred. The greatest number
that I killed, in any one season, of the same kind of animals,
was about one hundred and thirty.

In the month of June, 1801, my father with his family
removed to a more settled part of the country, twenty-two
miles down Pine Creek, near the west branch of the Susquehannah and within six miles of it. We took up our residence in an old barn, which was partly occupied by another
family. I thought I had left all my hunting; but we had
been there but a short time when we were told that a bear
was making havoc among the sheep, hogs, etc., in the neighborhood, and that he was as large as a cow. My father had
retained only two rifles, one for himself and one for me, and
kept but two of the hunting dogs, as he did not expect to
hunt much down there. One day, just as we had arisen from
dinner, we heard a hog squealing, and our neighbors informed
us that the bear had seized another hog. I took my gun,

and accompanied by one dog, started out to kill him. He was about one hundred rods off, walking on his hind feet with his back towards me, his fore paws firmly embracing the nearly dead hog, which weighed one hundred and forty pounds. He looked back occasionally as I approached him, and when I was within seventy yards of him, he dropped the hog and turned toward me, standing erect, and making, at the same time, a noise peculiar to the animal. I raised my gun, and taking aim at a white spot on his breast where the hair was parted, sent the ball through his heart. About the middle of August, we were reaping wheat on an island that my father owned, three-fourths of a mile above our residence, when a boy, who had been procuring water at a spring on the mainland, informed me that he had seen three bears crossing the creek above. Taking my rifle, which I always had with me when I went to work, I immediately started in pursuit, and soon had the satisfaction of shooting the largest of the three, but the others escaped, and I did not think it worth while to follow them.

About the middle of September, when the corn was sufficiently large for roasting, the bears were in the habit of coming to the island for it; we therefore took a number of poles sixteen feet long, placed them in the ground, and connecting the ends at the top secured them firmly with bark. A Dutchman, who was in my company, thatched it from bottom to top with rye straw, so that when finished, it had the appearance of a stack of straw. This house was for the purpose of concealing ourselves and dogs when the bears came to the island, so that we could surprise them suddenly. The first night we both watched, but did not kill anything. The next night the Dutchman watched alone and succeeded in killing a large bear. He asked me to watch with him the following night, which I refused to do, and he watched alone, but did not see any game. The next night I again refused to watch with him, it being Sunday. He said it was not best to let the bears eat the corn, and desired me to let him have my dog. I told him to let them have a little corn on Sunday. He watched but did not kill any. Three days afterwards he told me that he had not seen any signs of bears, but that the raccoons were troubling us; accordingly I watched with him, and we killed two in the evening and four at break of day. Our dogs would seize them and we would knock them in the head with a tomahawk, or take them by the tail and dash their heads against a tree. We did not watch again for some time.

One night my father said there was every appearance of raccoons having been in the fields. The Dutchman and I went out to hunt them, but returned unsuccessful. Sometime after that, he said he had seen the tracks of a large bear, which had torn down considerable corn, and as he expected the bear would return, he asked me to go with him and watch, but I declined doing so. He watched alone, undisturbed by the bear.

At this season, the bears subsisted principally on the chestnuts and acorns which were then ripening; so I told the Dutchman that if we hunted any more for bears we would go into the woods, as they generally laid still when there were nuts to eat. He coincided with me. A few weeks after that, another bear commenced his ravages among the corn which was in stacks; they would pull them down, making great havoc. The Dutchman and I pursued him with the dogs, came up with him, and the dogs worried him so that when he came to a fence he was unable to get over. We called them off and allowed him to pass over and go about half way across the stream between the island and main land, when we let our dogs go again. They caught him as he was leaving the water, and soon treed him. We did not dare to fire at him until morning, for should we only wound him he would come down and kill our dogs. I returned home, but Hans remained all night and at day-break shot the bear.

A few weeks after, we had a slight fall of snow, and I went out after bears, but found none, though I killed two deer; I skinned them and hung the venison up on such small poles that the bears could not climb, and out of reach of the wolves. About ten days after, more snow having fallen, we went out again, but returned home unsuccessful, and hunted no more until July, when the bears again commenced their depredation by killing a calf belonging to one of our neighbors, after which they killed several hogs. At that time the bears were traveling from the west to the east. The Dutchman and myself started out after the first and killed three which we had driven up a tree. By the first of August we had killed six. We did not hunt any except when they killed the hogs and sheep. On the tenth of August I went twenty-two miles up the creek to haul logs. We had to load them in the creek, near what was called a bear run-way. At this time the bears were going from east to west, and as they all crossed the creek at the same place, they stepped in the same track, so that it had the appearance of being the track of but one bear. Occasionally when there were three or four bears together, I would go down towards where they crossed and throw stones and clubs to drive them back; but I could never make them return up the hill; they would always go down the stream a short distance, and so gain the opposite shore, then come back on the bank to the old track. Every time I saw a bear I marked it down, and in a month I counted forty-three. I then went home, but returned to work again in about four days. The first bear that I saw after my return was a very large one — about as large as a common-sized cow, and the largest I ever saw. I thought I would see what I could do with him; so I waded into the water about knee deep, and commenced throwing stones at him. He paid no attention to them or me either, but kept on his course the same as though I had not been there. I was just beginning to think of retreating, when I thought I would throw one more; picking up a large stone, I threw it and hit him on the forehead. He raised himself on his hind feet, uttered a savage growl and rushed furiously towards me. I ran to the logs, caught up my axe and sprang upon a pair of timber wheels, which were eleven feet high. Before springing upon the wheels I looked around and saw him close at my heels. I raised my axe, intending to plunge it into his brain; but in the excitement missed my aim, and the handle struck his feet, which caused him to give another cry of pain. I was now on the wheels, and took off my hat and shook it at him, causing him to step back a little. I saw death staring me in the face. I knew their nature so well, and knew that if he got hold of me, he would not relinquish his hold until I was dead; but soon he began to move slowly off, looking around every few steps to observe my movements. When he had gone about two rods I started the oxen, which were hitched to the timber wheels, with a log loaded. As soon as I saw the bear strike the trail I got off and hastened to my brother's house, where I lived, to procure a gun. He had frightened me worse than I ever was before or since, and I wanted to take revenge. The house was a little more than half a mile distant, and I reached it in a very short time. When I arrived there, my sister inquired why I looked so pale, and if I was sick? I told her; and taking my gun, tomahawk, and a hunting knife, started in a direction to strike the trail about half a mile from the river, in hopes of meeting the gentleman and giving him a proper reception, but when I reached the river I found that he had passed. During the next six weeks they were not molested, and in that period I saw sixty-three, and my brother thirty-three, making ninety-six that were seen crossing, besides those that probably crossed unobserved. About the tenth of October they commenced crossing from the west to the east, making a trail across my father's island, which was planted to corn in five fields of ten acres each. The Dutchman and I made another house between the bank and a root, which served for two sides of the house. The first night we watched we were unsuccessful, and did not make another attempt for several nights. At length the Dutchman, another man and myself went out to watch. Three times in the night they rose and went out to look for them, but with no success. Just at break of day I awoke, went to the door, and saw a bear coming. Taking my gun and dog I stole out cautiously, leaving the others sleeping soundly. The dog gave chase, and stopped him as he had crossed the island and was about to plunge into the stream on the opposite side. Here was an abrupt bank of about eight feet, and as the bear attempted to descend this the dog would seize him and he would turn upon the dog. When I came up, the bear plunged off the bank, followed by the dog, which continued to worry him in the water. Seizing a moment when the bear turned to face the dog, I fired, killing him instantly. The men in the hut, hearing the report of my gun, ran out to see what was my success, but I drew the bear under the bank, where it could not be seen, and moved off a short distance. When they approached me, they asked me what I had shot. I replied that I guessed it was some one below. They did not believe this, but told me they thought I had killed a bear. I told them to come and see, leading them to where I had left my booty.

About two weeks after the last occurrence, a boy belonging to a neighboring family came to us saying that there were three bears in one of their corn-fields pulling down the corn, and requested me to come and kill them. I accordingly took my gun and rode over there. The old man and woman were mounted on stumps, watching the depredations of their un-welcome visitors, all three of which I dispatched without much difficulty. In two days I killed two more while they were crossing the creek. I now hunted until the middle of December, killing fourteen bears, and seventeen deer. When the ground was covered with snow I took a dog with me and treed them. When there was no snow I generally found them on the ground eating acorns and chestnuts. In February I was shown the tracks of two bears, which I followed to a hole in the rocks, in which they were concealed. The man who accompanied me went into the hole with a pole about twelve feet long, on the end of which was a lighted match. He penetrated as far as was prudent, threw in the match with all his force, and then hastened out. After waiting some time in vain for the bears to make their appearance, we both went in with a lighted match and a gun. After going in some distance, we found the opening so narrow that it was very difficult to proceed, and we threw in the match and beat a retreat. In about fifteen minutes we heard a rustling in the cave, and calling to my companion to stand clear, I stationed myself where I could shoot them as they emerged. As the first one made his appearance at the entrance, I fired, and he fell dead. The other one rushed out over him, and during the delay of reloading my gun, he obtained quite a start of me. I set the dog after him, and after chasing him two miles, he ran up a tree, and I shot him. This was the last I killed until the first of May, when I shot one which was very large and fat, having been but a short time out of its winter quarters. We estimated that it would weigh five hundred pounds. In June I shot one that was carrying off a hog. I hunted no more for about three years.

In 1800 I removed to Black Walnut Bottoms, and the next year I went fire-hunting, accompanied by a man named Clark. We pushed up the creek about five miles, when we made a fire and lay there until midnight. There was another party below us which had hunted down the river since nine o'clock without success. We started about half-past twelve o'clock. I sat in front for the first three miles, killing nothing, when I exchanged places with Clark. He had been seated forward but a short time when he said that he saw twenty deer, he could count them by their eyes. He observed that they were very long-legged, and held their heads remarkably high, for deer. As we floated nearer them we discovered that they were elk. We both leveled our rifles to fire together, but smoke from the torch blew into my face so that I could not see to take aim. Clark fired, however, and one of the elk leaped from the water, and fell heavily to the earth. Then ensued a scene which I shall never forget. The frightened animals rushed to the shore, and seeing their shadows on the bluff bank, in the flickering light of our torch, took them for new enemies, and turned again into the water, roaring so that the very earth seemed to tremble. They dashed down the stream, a few rods, clashing their hoofs and antlers together, then turned and again went to the shore a short distance below us. During the whole time I was so blinded by the smoke that it was impossible to use my rifle with any effect. As they approached the bank they were again frightened by the immense shadows moving in front of them, and dashing again into the water, they struck for the opposite shore. We lay directly in the course they took, and in the rush two of them leaped over the canoe beween Clark and myself, and a third ran against one end and overturned it. The light being extinguished, there was nothing to excite their fears, and they all ascended the bank, and made off. The water into which we were precipitated was about three feet deep, and we reached the shore without difficulty. We then righted our canoe and proceeded to bail out the water with our hats. As it was a very large one, this was a work of much labor. Our next object was to procure dry wood and make a fire, which, as the rain was now falling quite hard, was no easy matter. When Clark stepped upon the shore, he was met by the warning note of a large rattlesnake which lay coiled up at his feet. He returned to the canoe and proposed to float down to a more favorable place, but I told him I should not go farther in our present plight.

I made the next attempt to land, and met with a similar reception from another rattle-snake. I stepped to the canoe, pushed up the stream, and once more stepped ashore, beating about me with a stick to find whether there were snakes about, until I reached the top of the bank, which was about ten feet high. On the top I found a half-decayed pine stump, which leaned over in such a manner that the lower side was dry. Calling to Clark, and informing him what I had found, I proceeded to set fire to it. Fortunately, my powder had kept dry, and in a few minutes the stump was enveloped in a blaze. We then built a fire in our canoe, and pushed down the creek, arriving at home about daybreak. I told Clark he might have the elk we had killed, if he would go after it.

About ten days after, Clark and I started again on a fire-hunt. Pushing up the stream about seven miles, we turned and commenced floating down at nine o'clock. After proceeding about a mile, Clark, who sat forward, saw a large buck, a short distance ahead. He fired and wounded the animal, when it wheeled and attempted to plunge over the canoe. Clark held up his hand to protect himself, which frightened him still more, and he sprang across the canoe, giving Clark a blow between the eyes, with its hind feet, which knocked him prostrate. I asked him if he was hurt, and he replied that he was nearly killed. I pushed ashore as soon as possible, and took him out of the canoe. His face was bathed in blood, and presented a ghastly appearance. Upon washing away the blood I discovered that he was not as badly injured as I had feared. There was a severe contusion in the spot where he was struck, but the skin was not broken, and the blood had dropped from the wounded deer. I then went after the deer, which I found lying down, badly wounded, but not dead. I finished it by a ball through the head, and dragged it to the canoe. We floated down a mile, when we saw a buck and doe eating moss. Clark fired, killing the buck, and the doe ran ashore, when, becoming frightened at her shadow, she leaped back toward the canoe. As she raised to spring over, I hit her on the nose with a paddle, and she fell back into the canoe, when I cut her throat. We then floated down, picked up our buck, and proceeded homeward with three deer, one of which had not cost us even a shot.

About the first of the next December, I went on a bear-hunt, accompanied by a man named Hamlin. We soon treed and killed a large bear, which we dressed and hung up. In a short time we met two more, one of which we killed. We returned home, and the next morning started with a horse to convey home our bears, and before we reached them we killed another. This made a load for our horse, and we accordingly started at once for home, and the next day went for the first two. When we had loaded them and proceeded a short distance, we killed another, which we were compelled to leave and return for the next day.

About the middle of July, 1805, Morrison, Francis and myself were out on a hunt. Going up the creek about five miles, we commenced floating down, and soon shot a deer, which we stowed away in our canoe. When we had gone a short distance farther, two of us saw a deer in the stream, and both fired at the same time, but neither appeared to hit it. We re-loaded and directed the man who was steering to run the canoe to the shore. We then stood on the shore, about thirty rods from the deer, and each fired eight shots at it, as rapidly as we could load, when our guns became so hot that we were compelled to stop. The steersman had been holding up the torch for us to see by, yet the position of the animal was the same as when first observed. At each shot it had seemed to spring up, each time higher and higher, and dropping into the same spot. We now threw sticks at it, to drive it away, when it gave two or three leaps, and suddenly disappeared. This affair may appear somewhat strange to the reader, as it did to me, but the facts are as I have stated, and always appeared to me unaccountable.

CHAPTER XIII.

In November, 1817, William Gibson, Joseph Hook and myself started for the headwaters of the Kenzua Creek and Clarion River, to capture and bring home a live elk. They were to defray all the expenses and own one-half the elk when caught. They hired an Indian named George Silverheels, to assist, paying him a dollar a day. On arriving at the head waters of the Kenzua, we built a camp. Hook and myself then went to look for elk-tracks, leaving the others at the camp to cook provisions. About four miles northeast of the camp we found the tracks of quite a herd, which we followed for a mile and a half, when we found where twenty-nine had lain in the snow. We concluded to return to the camp, but it soon became dark, and we found it very difficult to follow our track back. We arrived there about eleven o'clock, and informed them that we had tracked twenty-nine. I told Silverheels, in Indian, that I thought they were all middling-sized does and fawns, and did not think there was one we would wish to catch. The following day, each man carrying provisions for six days, we set out, accompanied by four dogs. About ten o'clock we reached the elk-beds. I told them that we should find them not more than two miles ahead, and proposed that one should go ahead and kill a couple of them, and the others remain behind with the dogs. They desired me to go and when I had proceeded about three-quarters of a mile I discovered about ten elk. I raised my rifle, but it had become wet in coming through the snow, and having a flint lock, would not go. I tried three times, when the elk became alarmed, and I waited for the others to arrive. I told Silverheels that my gun was wet, and if his was in order, to follow with the dogs, and if they stopped the elk, to kill one. They all went on, leaving me to unbreech my gun. I worked at it about half an hour, unsuccessfully, when, as the snow was falling very rapidly, and I feared to lose the track, I started after the others, overtaking them about seven

miles distant. I soon heard the barking of the dogs, and told
Silverheels he had better go on ahead, while we would remain,
lest so many should alarm the elk. When we heard the report of his rifle we went to him, and found that he had
killed an elk. Silverheels and myself continued on the trail,
leaving the others to dress the elk and prepare a camp for the
night. When we had proceeded three-quarters of a mile, we
found one of the dogs and an elk which Silverheels shot. It
was now quite dark, and we left it and went back to the
others. They had stretched the skin of the elk across poles
to form a shelter, but could not succeed in making a fire
outside, and were compelled to light one under the skin.
The snow was falling rapidly, which rendered it extremely
difficult, and it was not until one o'clock that we finally succeeded. In the meantime we suffered severely from the cold.
At daylight the snow had fallen to the depth of four feet,
and it was with much labor that we beat down the snow
sufficiently to procure wood. We were unable to reach the
elk which we had left out, until the second day, when we
dressed and brought it into the camp. We remained there
three days, drying our venison, and tramping down the snow,
but were unable to go a great distance from the camp. The
fourth day it thawed sufficiently to settle the snow a few
inches, and we left our camp, and after toiling through the
snow all day, encamped at night seven miles from our start-
ing-place. The following day we traveled nine miles farther,
reaching our old camp. We remained here three days, waiting for a thaw. I told the others that I thought we might
find two or three large elk near where we had started the
small ones. Silverheels and Gibson objected to the idea of
going after them in the snow, but Hook consented to go
with me. The following day we went four miles, and found
the tracks of three large elk, which had passed the day before. We followed them half a mile, and found them on the
side of a hill, eating moss. They were large, noble animals,
and each one would have been worth five hundred dollars if
we could have taken them. We thought it best not to attempt this, without the rest of the party and the dogs, and
accordingly returned without disturbing them, reaching the
camp about nine o'clock, greatly fatigued. Gibson and Silverheels awoke on our arrival, and inquired what luck. Hook
replied that we had started three fine elk, worth five hundred
dollars each. Upon this they became quite animated, and
Gibson said he would chase them two weeks, if necessary

to catch one. I told him he might follow them a month without taking one, if the dogs would not go. The next morning all set out, and at eleven o'clock arrived at the place where we had left the elk, when I went on in advance, the others following at the distance of a hundred yards. I soon saw the elk, and halted till the others came up. They loosed the dogs, but it was difficult for them to run through the deep snow, and the elk gained upon them. I said it was useless for us to make any further attempt, as the dogs would soon return; but the others were eager to follow them, and my objections were overruled. We followed them three miles, when two of them struck off to the west, the other keeping on a straight course, with the dogs after it. After going another mile the dogs returned. It was now between three and four o'clock, and we were all heartily discouraged. Silverheels said it was useless to go farther, as the dogs would not go through the deep snow, which I had told them before. They asked me what I thought it best to do. I told them that as it was near night, we had better make a hemlock shanty, and stay there over night, which we did, and passed the night very comfortably. In the morning they again asked my opinion about our next movements, and I told them we could do nothing until the snow had settled so that the dogs could run. We returned to our camp and waited two days for a thaw, but the weather became colder, and we concluded to go home. When we had arrived within six miles of Kenzua, Gibson gave out and could go no farther. We made him a fire, and when we reached the settlement, we sent back a man and horse to bring him in. This was the second time that I failed to take an elk alive, after having attempted it, and in this case we should have probably succeeded, had we not been prevented by the deep snow.

In August, 1820, I left Kenzua Flats, in company with John Campbell and Robert McKean, for the headwaters of the Susquehannah River, to take an elk. We hired two Indians, named Morris Halftown and John Geebuck, with a pack-horse, to assist us. I had never taken an elk alive, in summer, but with good dogs I thought we might, as they would be most likely to flee to a creek or river. I had killed many that I might have caught if I had attempted it. We encamped the first night on a small stream flowing into the Kenzua, seventeen miles above the Kenzua Flats. The following day Campbell, myself, and the two Indians went to look for elk-tracks, each taking a different direction, leav-

ing McKean to keep camp, take care of the horse, and cook.
We all returned at twelve o'clock, as had been agreed upon
except Halftown, who came in about half-past one, having,
about nine miles from the camp started seven doe elk and
fawns, and killed one of them. We all went to secure the
one he had killed, arriving there about dark. Campbell and
the two Indians skinned the elk, while McKean cut wood,
and I went in search of water. When I returned they had
dressed the elk, and we cut up and salted it in the skin. The
following day Halftown and Geebuck went down Stump
Creek to look for signs of elk. If they found the tracks
of large ones they were to return and inform us, but if small
they were to follow and kill some. They took a supply of
salt, with which to cure the meat of any they might kill at
a distance from the camp. Campbell, McKean and myself
made a scaffold upon which to dry our meat, and when done
we spread out the meat, and Campbell and myself went
to hunt a camping-ground near a large lick, leaving McKean
to dry the venison. We found a suitable place about half
a mile above the lick, where we built a camp. The following morning we returned to where we had left McKean, loaded the horse with our dried venison, and waited until noon
for the Indians to come in, when, as they had not arrived,
we marked our road so that they could find us, and went to
the other camp. The Indians joined us that evening. They
had seen some signs of elk, that had passed some days before,
but no fresh ones. The next morning they again departed
in direction of the Susquehannah and Stump Creek, to look
for elk, and should they find does or small bucks they were
to kill as many as possible. Campbell and myself started with
three days provisions and two dogs, leaving McKean in the
camp to take care of the horse. We went south toward the
head of the Tionesta, and about three o'clock came where
two bucks had passed the day before. Judging by the tracks
they were about three years old. They were heading toward
the lick near which we had encamped. We followed till
evening, and encamped on the trail. Next morning after
going four miles we found them. We let loose the dogs,
and they went off after the elk at a rapid rate, heading toward
the Kenzua. We followed as fast as possible, thinking to
catch one of them in some deep hole in the creek. We kept
on the track to the creek, found that the elk had gone down
the stream, sometimes in the water and sometimes on the
shore. We followed on for two miles, when we met our

dogs returning. It being a very warm day, we returned, discouraged, to our camp near the elk lick. I told Campbell that with six dogs, if they were not better than these, we could not catch an elk, as they would not keep on the track. When we arrived at the camp, we found the Indians there, but the horse had strayed away. It was now Saturday night, and Campbell said that he did not wish to hunt horses on the Sabbath. I said that it was not a day for such business, but in this case I considered it a work of necessity, as he might stray so far before Monday as to be lost beyond recovery. I offered to go with the Indians, and leave the other two at the camp. We started early the following day, and when we had gone a short distance I directed Halftown to take the Smithport and Warren road, where he could easily track it if it had been there, as there was no travel on it at that season, and if it had gone home, to follow and bring it back to the camp as soon as possible. Geebuck and myself went to where McKean had left the horse, and followed his tracks across the Kenzua and up a high mountain. When we reached the top of the mountain I told Geebuck that if he would follow on and bring the horse to the camp I would give him a dollar extra. I then went toward Tuneangwant creek and then back to the camp, without having seen anything of the horse. Halftown was there without the horse, and soon after dark Geebuck arrived. He said that he had followed the tracks ten or eleven miles to a dry, rocky ridge, where they could no longer be distinguished. He accordingly marked the place and returned to the camp. Monday morning Campbell set out with Geebuck in search of the horse, while McKean, Halftown and myself went to hunt for elk. We took the dogs and a supply of provisions for four days, going toward Stump Creek. When we had proceeded seven miles it commenced raining, and we hastily constructed a shelter, under which we remained until the next morning. We then went southeast to a small stream which we mistook for the Tionesta Creek. We soon saw signs of elk, although made some days before. The tracks indicated large animals, and they followed the ridge by the side of the stream. We followed the creek several miles still thinking it was the Tionesta, until we arrived at a place where some trees had been peeled, by which Halftown knew the creek to be the southeast branch of the Kenzua, and that he and his father had peeled that bark twelve years before, and with it built a shanty, in which they had wintered. We encamped here for the night, and in the morning resolved to give up the pursuit and return home, thinking it quite probable that Campbell and Geebuck had done so. We arrived at Kenzua at the same time with Campbell and Geebuck, but the horse had not been found. We went to Campbell's house, where we took dinner and settled our affairs, after which we sent the Indians back to camp for our meat, cooking utensils, etc. We paid sixty dollars for the horse, which with the provisions, wages of the Indians, and loss of our own time made the total loss one hundred and twenty-six dollars, being forty-two dollars each. McKean had agreed, in case we failed to secure an elk, to assist me in building, half a day for each day I lost. The great cause of the failure of our expedition was the want of good dogs.

I will now give a short description of the mountains and streams between Warren to Olean, on the east side of the river, where I on[c]e hunted elk, bears, panthers and sables. My first elk-hunting in this region was in 1816, and I continued it for five years. During this time I traveled over every part of this section of Pennsylvania and New York, and became familiar with the country between the Allegany and Susquehannah. In a circuit of ten miles around the head of the Tionesta, I thought the pine timber was better than in any other part of the region I have mentioned. The timber region commenced about seven miles from the Allegany river, two miles above Warren. The southeast branch heads in a good farming country, covered with beech, maple, chestnut, and some scattering wild-cherry trees, some of which latter measured three feet in diameter, and not a branch within fifty feet of the ground. Here were also white-wood trees, four feet in diameter, with the lower limbs sixty feet from the ground. The country round the mouth of the creek was covered with a magnificent growth of pine and oak. Hence to the head of Willow Creek is a good farming country, covered with oak, chestnut, beech, maple, and a sprinkling of pine, hemlock and wild cherry. Around the head of the Tuneangwant creek and on the south side is also a good farming country. I never hunted on the north side, but have been told that it is as good a country for farming purposes as the south side. From the Quaker Run to the head of Tuneangwant, thence to Sugar Run, Kenzua Creek, and on to the Tionesta, I have been familiar, and know it to be good farming land. On the north branch of the Kenzua I have seen indications of stone-coal and have no doubt

[87]

there are large deposits of it in that vicinity, as well as around the head of Willow Creek. Six miles from the mouth of Kenzua Creek, on the north side, is good land for cultivation. Also, up Sugar Run, about the same distance from the Allegany, is a fine tract of land. East from the head of Stump Creek I think the land is not quite as valuable for farming as it is farther north, toward the state line, beyond which it is excellent. From the source of Stump Creek the land is good for about ten miles, when the surface becomes very uneven, as it is near the river, on most of the streams. Between the Kenzua and Stump Creek I have seen cherry trees from two to three feet in diameter, straight, and nearly sixty feet to the first branch. White-wood is also interspersed through this region, of the finest quality, and growing to an immense size. Groves of small cherry trees, from six to fifteen inches in diameter, were quite numerous, and similar groves of white ash were often met with in places where the first growth had been prostrated by the wind.

CHAPTER XIV.

HUNTING AND TRAPPING.

IN November, 1821, in company with Walter Seaman, John Campbell and George Morrison, I went on a general hunting expedition to catch elk, hunt bears, deer and panthers, and to trap foxes and sables. We hired a man named Goodwin, with a horse, to act as porter to the expedition, and Marshall Whitcomb as cook and camp-keeper. We were six in all, in a double sleigh. Having gone about six miles we found the tracks of a panther. I told Seaman and Goodwin that I must go with the sleigh, and that they should follow the tracks, and if they did not come up with the panther in two or three miles to return and they would find me encamped at night about three miles ahead. Campbell and Morrison were forward, and Whitcomb had charge of the dogs. Seaman and Goodwin took two dogs with them and followed the track, finding it nearly parallel with the road. They had proceeded but two miles when the panther came out from under some rocks. Seaman fired and brought him down. I heard the gun and called out to them. They answered, and soon I saw them drag out a very large panther, weighing about two hundred pounds, and place it on the sleigh. Proceeding on we found Morrison and Campbell making a fire for us; they had not killed anything. We there encamped for the night and arranged our hunting matters. The next morning Morrison hunted on the north side of the road, Seaman on the south side and I went on in the road, telling them that I would stand as good a chance as either of them. We were all to meet at four corners about seven miles beyond and encamp that night. Three miles ahead was an open beech woods on the side of a hill down which the road passed; and in the road, at the bottom of the hill, trotting along towards me, I saw nine wolves. I stepped behind a large beech tree and waited their approach. A large tree with the leaves on had fallen across the road about twenty rods from me, and the

wolves came up and stopped behind it, so that I could but
partially see one of them. I fired at him and he rolled over
once or twice and then got up and ran west. I followed him,
but he would skulk around in the tops of fallen trees and
thickets. I fired at him three times at a great distance but
did not succeed in killing him. I followed him until three
o'clock in the afternoon and it was night before I arrived
at the place where I first shot at him. Then I had seven
miles further to go after dark to our encampment at the
four corners, which I reached about eleven o'clock, very
tired. During the night snow fell ten inches deep, and of
course covered the wolf's tracks, which prevented me from
following him the next day, when I should probably have
found him dead. During the day Goodwin returned to Kenzua with the horses and sleigh, and was to come back with
but one of the horses. That morning Morrison and Whitcomb set forty sable traps, called dead-falls; they were so
constructed that when the sable came to eat the bait a small
log would fall and kill him. Seaman, Campbell and myself,
with two dogs, went forth on a hunt. We crossed the Kenzua, and going south about twelve miles, found the fresh
tracks of a large sized elk, which we followed one mile and
found its bed of the night previous. We remained with the
dogs, and Campbell went ahead about a hundred rods, when
he saw a fine buck elk. He called to us to let the dogs go;
we did so, and the elk ran north toward Smethport, about
nine miles, and stopped on a rock. A deer pursued by two
wolves, passing near the rock, so frightened our dogs that
they left the elk and made for the camp. When we arrived
and saw the wolves tracks we mistook them for those of
our dogs, thinking they had gone after the deer. We followed down the creek eleven miles to a settlement, and inquiring
for the dogs, were told that two wolves had brought in a
deer, but that they had not seen any dogs. We could not
credit this story, and searched until three o'clock, thinking
that the inhabitants had concealed them. Seaman and Campbell returned to the camp, leaving me to keep up the search
for the dogs. The next day I went up Potato creek, where
a man said he had seen a handsome black hound, which I
thought must be ours. All day I searched for the dogs up
the creek, and passed the night twelve miles from the settlement, still under the impression that the inhabitants had
concealed them. The next day I went to Smethport, and there
found a man who said there were people enough in the vicin-

ity that would hide my dogs. I hired him to assist me in my search, but of course we were unsuccessful. I remained at Smethport that night, and the next day returned to the camp, but found no one there except the dogs that I had lost. I knew then that the wolves had frightened the dogs from the elk. In the evening the rest of the party came in from hunting. I found that during our absence Morrison had killed three deer, and Whitcomb had caught ten sables; Campbell and Seaman had also each killed a deer since they arrived. I inquired why they did not go elk hunting, as they had all the dogs with them? Seaman replied that if the dogs had stopped twenty elk, they could not have caught one, for none but me could rope one. I said that perhaps they could and perhaps not, but it might be that I could not do so myself. I told them that they must prepare for another campaign. The next day I remained at the camp to bake bread, and the rest hunted. I baked it in the ashes, and having good success, finished by two o'clock. Then I took my gun and went about a mile and a half, and came to the tracks of seven deer. I followed them half a mile and found the deer lying in a thicket. I got upon a log to see them, when a large doe jumped up. I fired and broke her shoulder blade. She ran, her fawn after her; and by the time I had loaded my gun and was prepared to follow, Seaman's dog, who had gnawed his rope and broke loose, came up and put off on the track. I followed them about a mile, but it was so late that I returned to the camp, where I arrived at eight o'clock. The dog caught the deer and did not return for three days, but when he came he looked fat and sleek, having eaten the deer. When I arrived at the camp they inquired what luck I had. I told them that if it had not been for Seaman's dog, I would have had a fine doe, for I had wounded it and it could not have gone far before I should have shot it.

I told them we must hunt for elk the next day, and that they must build another camp on the south side of the Kenzua, six miles from the main stream and twelve or fourteen miles from the old camp, as I did not believe that there were any more elk on the west side of the creek, where we were now stationed. This they agreed to; but thought that Goodwin (who had now got back with his horse) and Whitcomb had better go and make the camp, and the rest start immediately after the elk. We took four dogs with us and were loaded with four days provisions. Crossing the Kenzua, we went southwest about twelve miles, and found the tracks

of seven elk, which we followed three miles and then encamped for the night. The next morning we followed them
five miles and found the fresh tracks of the same elk returning. I said it was no use to try to take one alive, for
they were all does and young elk, and that we had better try
to kill them. Morrison and Seaman said they wanted to
be the ones to go on. So they went and we stayed behind
with the dogs. They were told to whistle if the elk saw
them and run so that they could not get a shot, and we
would let the dogs go. They had not gone more than a hundred yards when we heard them whistle. We let the dogs
loose and they stopped the herd about a mile distant. Morrison and Seaman came up with them in a few minutes and
shot three. After we had dressed them, Morrison and Seaman
wished to take the dogs and attempt to kill one or two more,
but I was afraid the dogs would not run, in consequence
of having been fed too much. The four elk ran together
about two miles, when three of them turned off to one side,
and all the dogs but mine returned. The men followed the
other dog and elk twelve miles, when they saw the dog lying
down beside a large log, and supposed that he had lain down
to rest, and of course thought the elk had gone on; but when
Morrison called to the dog, " Hunter, have you given out? "
he sprang over the log, gave a yelp and up jumped the elk.
It was so tired, however, that it did not go more than twenty
rods before Morrison killed it. One of the men procured fuel
whilst the other skinned the elk. They stretched the skin
on poles, made a fire near it but passed a very uncomfortable
night, as it snowed quite hard. The next morning, taking
their elk skin with them, they started for the place where
Campbell and myself had made quite a comfortable encampment, arriving about eleven o'clock. I told them I thought
instead of having our new camping place on the Kenzua, we
had better make it on a road called the Kittaning road, as
we should not have so far to carry our game, to which the
others assented. Seaman then obtained permission to go home
and remain about a week, and the following day we proceeded
by way of the Kittaning road, to our encampment near the
Four Corners. On our road we found an old log house, which
was built at the time the road was made. The roof had fallen
in, but we decided to repair and make it our headquarters.
Whitcomb had caught twenty-three sables, and Morrison had
killed two deer. That night, for the first time in three weeks,
our whole party was together. The following day Morrison

and Seaman went home, and the remainder of us proceeded to the Kittaning block-house, which we fitted up for use. Next day Goodwin brought in the three elk which had been killed, and after dinner Campbell, Morrison and myself went to hunting, and Whitcomb to set sable traps. After hunting until the afternoon of the next day, we found the track of a single elk, which we judged to be a young buck. We followed it seven miles and then stopped for the night. The next morning we were early on the trail, and about ten o'clock we found the tracks quite fresh, and knowing the animal could not be far away, we let loose the dogs, which soon came up with him. He ran near our second camp, keeping a west course. In his course he passed a fox-trap which I had set several days before, and in passing, I discovered that a large fox was in the trap. I dispatched him with my tomahawk, and left him in the trap. The elk, still keeping west, crossed two small branches of the Kenzua, and the Smethport road, and then, turning north, ascended a mountain, stopping on a rock about twenty-five feet high. We did not arrive until nine o'clock, when, on approaching the elk, I observed to my chagrin that it was a doe. I communicated my discovery to Morrison, who had the gun, and he shot her. We then went down to the Tuneangwant, and encamped. It was after midnight when we had our arrangements completed, and soon after a furious storm of hail and snow set in which covered the earth to the depth of two feet, before morning. The following day we skinned the elk, and hung up the meat where it was killed. We then remained there a day and a half, waiting for more favorable weather.

The third day the weather became somewhat more propitious, and we set out for the camp at the Corners, finding it very difficult traveling, as the snow was three feet deep. We arrived there about nine o'clock that evening, nearly exhausted, from toiling through the deep snow. Campbell and Morrison were discouraged, believing it useless to attempt catching an elk while the snow was so deep, and the next morning we started for home, arriving at my house at Cold Spring late at night. The next day I returned to Kenzua, and offered Morrison and Campbell my share of every thing but the sable skins if they would bring home the meat and skins. They did not wish to go, and accordingly I went alone to the Kittaning block-house, where I found Seaman, Whitcomb and Goodwin, with forty sable skins and the meat of four elk. The next day Whitcomb and Goodwin conveyed to Kenzua the meat of the fifteen deer we had killed, while Seaman and myself remained behind, resolved, if possible, to catch an elk. The next day at noon it began to thaw, and we set out with two of our best dogs, in search of tracks. We returned to our block-house that evening. Seaman felt considerably disheartened and proposed that we should give up the hunt and go home. I could not abandon the idea of making one more effort, and to encourage my companion I told him of my success two years before, when I took two elk in less than a month, and received as my share three hundred and sixty dollars. This gave him new animation, and he said he would stick by me as long as there was a flake of snow to track them by. The following day, when we had proceeded about four miles we found some large tracks which had been made about the time of the hail-storm. We followed them until about three o'clock, when he concluded that they must have gone to the rocks at the head of Marvin's Creek, and decided to return to our block-house, and in the morning endeavor to strike the trail between that place and the creek. The next day we found the track about three o'clock, and followed until night when we made a comfortable camp. Our spirits for the past day had not flagged, and now that we seemed so near the object of our long and weary hunt, we felt impatient for the morning, feeling confident that we should secure our prize before another night. Indeed, we had already sold him in imagination, and each was counting on his share of the thousand dollars it might bring, while the lowest figure was not less than three hundred dollars. We arose in the morning in high spirits, took a hasty breakfast, and by daylight were on the track. About eight o'clock the snow began to fall very rapidly, and soon obliterated every vistage of the trail. But the icy sheet did not lie colder upon the earth that it did upon our hopes. We followed on in the best way we could until noon, when it was impossible to proceed farther, and we encamped. By night the weather cleared up, and the cold became intense. The following night was the coldest one we experienced that winter. The next day we decided to return home. We proceeded to the Kenzua, which we descended on the ice to the Kittaning road about three miles from the Corners, and then went to our first camp, where we staid that night. We there struck a balance of the profit and loss of the expedition. The wages of the men amounted to thirty dollars; provision for ourselves and provender for the horse fifteen dollars; a dog had been lost which had cost ten dollars; making a total expense fifty-five dollars, besides our time. Of the four partners to the expedition, two were out a month, and other two five weeks, making in all one hundred and twenty-six days. The receipts were forty sable-skins and fifteen deer-skins at seventy-five cents each; the panther's head brought a bounty of six dollars, in all forty-seven dollars and forty-five cents; which, with the venison, was all we obtained. The next day we returned home. On our arrival at Kenzua I gave my share of venison and elk-skins in the woods to my partners, as I resided at such a distance that I did not think they would pay for the trouble of conveying home.

In October, 1823, in company with John Campbell, Marshall Whitcomb and a Mr. Whitmore, I set out from Kenzua, in a large canoe, of above three tons burthen, to hunt and fish down the Allegany. We took with us four dogs and a seine. At the Big Bend, three miles below Kenzua, we took several barrels of fish of various kinds, among which were salmon, muskelonge, and some remarkably fine specimens of pike as well as white and yellow bass. We proceeded down to Glade Run, two miles above Warren, where we caught two barrels of fish and killed a fawn and buck deer. At the village we caught another barrel of fish. At Dunn's Eddy, nine miles below Warren, we killed two deer, but took no fish. One of the deer was a spike buck — the antlers running up straight, without branches. Three miles below, at the residence of Robert Thompson, we caught two barrels of fish, among which were some immense muskelonge; and also killed five deer. We then moved down about fourteen miles, to White Oak Shoot, where we shot two deer. Returning from our hunt, we again went to fishing with our seine, assisted by a resident there, named Daniel Jones, and three of his sons. Here we had a large haul, the weight of the fish being so great as to break the seine. The water being very clear, we could see an immense number of fish in the seine; not less, as we judged, than thirty barrels. I jumped in where the water was three feet deep, and held one side of the seine, while Jones held the other, but in spite of all our efforts, two-thirds of the fish escaped. We secured, however, about ten barrels. The seine was so badly torn that it occupied three of us nearly a day to repair it; while so engaged Whitmore, Campbell and the boys went out with the dogs and killed three deer. On drawing the net again, the fish had all disappeared; and we caught but twenty or thirty.

At Horse Creek, seventeen miles below, we killed two deer. That evening I was at Oil Creek, three miles below, and there I heard that two men named Carns, had threatened, if we hunted any farther down the river, to shoot our dogs, tar and feather me, and then, if the others did not leave the vicinity, to treat them to a coat of the same. I told my informant that I should come down there and hunt, and give the Carns an opportunity of executing their threat, if they could; but I thought it was a game at which two could play. I considered their interference entirely uncalled for, unless I killed a deer on their own land. Mrs. Holiday, who kept a tavern for raftsmen, said they were ugly men, and advised me to keep away, as she was unwilling to have an old customer injured. The next day the Carns went down to Franklin, five miles below their residence, and said that a man named Tome, and two others, were hunting down the river, killing all the deer, and that they would tar and feather him, kill his dogs and send him home, if he came any farther down. They asked a man named Thomas Hewling, who kept a tavern there, what sort of a man Tome was. Hewling said he was a good-natured sort of man, but if they attempted any violence they would find trouble, as he was a stout, active man, and not easily frightened. Campbell was rather timid, and thought we had better leave the vicinity. I told him that I should hunt there one day, at least, to see what they would do. Whitmore went off with the dogs in search of deer, and I told them if they would hunt down the river to Franklin I would join them there at night. Whitmore proceeded to hunt on one side of the river, and I on the other, within fifty rods of the house of one of the Carns. Before I had been there a long time, Carns came out and asked if I was hunting in their vicinity. I replied that I was, as game was more abundant there than where I lived. He said that he would join me a short time, and I told him that I had no objection to his taking an equal chance with me. Whitmore killed a deer in the water, and drove another into the river which Carns shot, and we divided it equally with him. On our arrival at Franklin we found Campbell there, with a large buck which he had killed. The next day we killed in that vicinity three deer, the following another, and the next day two more, when we started homeward. While going home, the water was so high that we did not try to fish, except in one place, where we obtained over one hundred fine salmon. We killed, during the hunt, sixty-seven deer. This was my last hunting expedition.

CHAPTER XV.

I HAVE found the favorite haunt of bears to be in Lycoming county, above Pine Creek, on the head waters of Larry's Creek, and on the first fork of Pine Creek. I have also found them near the head of Kettle Creek, Cedar Run, and Young Woman's Creek. In the month of August they were to be found traveling west, and crossing Pine Creek, twenty-four miles from the mouth, where they had a beaten road that might be followed fifteen or twenty miles. At that time the bears were lean and their skins were worthless, we did not, therefore wish to kill them. I have noticed that generally every seventh year the bears travel west in August, and return about the middle of October, but scattering wide apart and paying no attention to the path. I have also noticed that the winter succeeding the season in which they travel west is a very hard one. In severe winters the bears retire to the holes that they last occupied, whether it is ten, thirty or sixty miles distant, and when started they go in a straight course, not stopping for mountains, rivers or other obstructions, and when one is seen traveling in a direct line, without stopping, it is pretty certain that he is on his way to his hole. In very open winters they remain but a week or two in their holes. In more severe winters when they lie long in their holes the usual method is to smoke them out. After ascertaining by the tracks, or by entering the holes, that they are within, a cloth is covered with a mixture of lard and sulphur, ignited and inserted on a pole as far as possible. The fumes of the burning sulphur will soon drive forth any bears that may be concealed there, two or three, sometimes taking up their quarters in one den. It is well to have a dog along, as in case of there being more than one bear the dog will prove useful in driving one of them up a tree. I have mentioned this manner of hunting bears in another place, but as I am about explaining their nature and habits, it might not be out of place to repeat it here. Many suppose that the bear is constantly on the move, because seldom seen at rest. The reason of this is that when one who is not a hunter finds a bear, the animal has seen him first, and moves off, while he supposes that the bear was in motion before discovered. The truth is that from the middle of May until the same time in August, the bear sleeps as much as any other animal. I have seen them during the day sleeping by a log or among the brakes, and occasionally I have surprised and killed a bear while asleep, but not often, as they are worthless at this season. They are very voracious, and this often tempts them into the settlements for forage, and renders them an easy prey to traps and bear-houses. When he obtains sight or scent of any thing he desires, he takes it, regardless of traps, and thus falls an easy prey. I have described the manner of constructing bear-houses, in another chapter. When berries and nuts are to be found, he does not leave the woods, but in the absence of these he helps himself without ceremony to any sheep, calf or hog that may come within his reach. If a bait is hung even within a few rods of a dwelling, they will come for it, if they scent it. In one instance a bear took a hog weighing one hundred and fifty pounds from a sty within four rods of the dwelling. The bear came in the early part of the evening, and broke down the roof of the sty, the hog protesting so loudly against the proceeding that the man in the house heard his squeals, but suspecting the cause, he did not dare venture out and face the bear, as he had no gun. About half an hour after, I passed the place, and the man informed me of what had occurred. I told him he should have attacked the bear with an axe, if he had no gun. He replied that he did not wish to risk himself in such company, without a good weapon. On my way I passed the residence of a young man whom I sent back with a gun. The two went in pursuit of the bear, and found him feasting on the hog, in a thicket, not more than twenty-five rods from the house. They fired and the bear rushed with a loud growl out of the thicket. Men and dogs took to their heels, but on visiting the spot in the morning the bear was found dead. He was very large, and the skin was valuable, and as he had only made a beginning upon the hog, his hide and carcass more than paid for the damage he had done. About the first of November is the rutting season for bears, and at this time the old he-bears keep up a noise which may be heard a mile.

They are very fond of honey, and when one finds a bee-tree, he will not rest until he has obtained the honey. Once while I was in the woods hunting I heard a noise like that made by a bear while in a tree after nuts. It seemed somewhat strange, as it was not the season for nuts, and after reconnoitering for some time, I discovered a bear high up on a dead pine tree, scratching and pawing at the wood very industriously. I resolved to ascertain the cause of his strange conduct, and seated myself, where I could see the performance. In about half an hour he had penetrated the shell, and thrusting in his paws he brought them out loaded with honey. The bees flew at him, stinging his head, paws and tongue. He rubbed his head with his reeking paws, but did not allow the stings to interrupt his feast for a moment. He continued to gorge himself, and growl his impotent rage at his little tormentors, until I had witnessed enough, when I called loudly to him. He looked at me, but was so intent upon his repast that he paid but little attention. I repeated my call and swung my hat, when he comprehended the nature of the inturder, and letting go his hold he dropped to the ground, and made a precipitate retreat. I allowed him to move away unmolested, as the skin and flesh were worthless, it not being the season for them, and I did not wish to kill him out of mere wantonness. The bear has an instinctive fear of man, and unless wounded will always flee from his presence. When wounded they will fight with a desperation which renders it perilous to attack them. Once while out on a deer-hunt, my wanderings having led me to a grove of tall cherry-trees, I heard a crackling and rustling overhead. After looking and listening awhile I perceived a bear in a lofty cherry-tree, gathering the fruit, it being the season when it was ripe. He would break and drop to the earth the large limbs which were covered with fruit, watching each limb until it reached the ground, and if one lodged on a lower branch, he went down and liberated it. I observed his proceedings for fifteen or twenty minutes, and then concealing myself behind a tree, I called to him at the top of my voice. If a sudden shock of an earthquake had prostrated the tree in which he was stationed, Bruin could not have experienced more astonishment than he exhibited at the sound of my voice, breaking the stillness of the forest. He raised himself erect upon his haunches and stood looking eagerly around with a ludicrous mixture of astonishment and defiance. I stepped out from my concealment, and again

called, when, with a loud cry of terror, he slipped off the
limb, but while still grasping it with his fore paws he looked
to the ground. The tree leaned over a small precipice, and
if he relinquished his hold he must fall at least a hundred
feet. He hung there apparently balancing the matter in his
mind, for a few minutes, when his dread of man prevailed,
and gradually relaxing his hold, he fell heavily to the earth,
rolled up like a ball. He quickly recovered from the shock,
and straightening himself out, he made the best possible use
of his legs, and was soon out of sight. I allowed him to escape unharmed for the same reason as the one last mentioned.
With many I am aware this would not be considered sufficient reason for permitting a bear to escape, after having it
in my power, but I never wantonly killed an animal, when
I could gain nothing by its destruction. From October to
May their skins are good, and at this season I always killed
all I could. With a true hunter it is not the destruction of
life which affords the pleasure of the chase; it is the excitement attendant upon the very uncertainty of it which induces men even to leave luxurious homes and expose themselves to the hardships and perils of the wilderness. Even
when, after a weary chase, the game is brought down, he
cannot, after the first thrill of triumph, look without a
pang of remorse, upon the form which was so beautifully
adapted to its situation, and which his hand has reduced
to a mere lump of flesh. But with us, who made our homes
in the wilderness, there was a stronger motive than love of
excitement for seeking out and destroying the denizens of
the forest. We did it in obedience to the primal law of nature: for the subsistence or defence of ourselves and those
whom we were bound by the ties of nature to support and defend. When neither of these demanded the destruction of
an animal, I never felt any desire to harm it. It is often
dangerous to meet an old she-bear with her cubs, although
the old one will endeavor to escape with her young, but the
simple creatures will often come directly up to a man when
they meet him, and the enraged dam will attack him with a
fury which leaves him no hope but in his weapon. If he attempts to flee, the cubs will follow him, which increases the
rage of the old bear. A few years since, I was near the south
bank of the Allegany river, in Cattaraugus county, New
York, examining a road which had been made for drawing
logs, when I observed three black animals approaching me,
but thinking they were hogs, I paid no attention to them.

When I again looked in the same direction they were but a short distance from me, and I perceived that it was a bear with two cubs. I was somewhat alarmed, as I knew the ferocity of a bear when with her young, but knowing there was no chance for flight, I seized a handspike and prepared to defend myself the best I could. As the bear came near she raised herself erect and advanced with open mouth. When she was within reach I prostrated her by a blow upon the back. She fell upon one of her cubs, injuring it severely. This enraged her still more, and she sprang up and again rushed at me. I struck her on the head, and she fell again. She rose and slowly retired with the wounded cub. The other cub ran off in another direction, and I attempted to capture it, but it continually eluded me just as I had it almost within my grasp. After chasing it nearly half a mile I finally succeeded in taking it by throwing my coat over it. It was but a little larger than a good-sized cat, and I carried it home in a basket which I borrowed of an Indian who lived in the vicinity. When a bear is attacked and wishes merely to act upon the defensive, it stands erect and with its fore-paws repels the attack. If it wishes to close in with the enemy, it grasps it with its fore-paws, while with its teeth and hind-paws it tears its victims to pieces. I know of but one animal ranging our forests which I think capable of defending itself successfully against a bear — that is a buck elk with full-grown antlers. I never knew of a contest between a bear and an elk, but I have no doubt the elk would prove more than a match. Bears seldom fight among themselves, and I never witnessed but one instance of a conflict between two of them. It was in November, a light snow lay upon the ground, and in wandering through the woods I struck the tracks of three bears. After following them some distance I arrived at a place which had evidently been the scene of a desperate encounter. The snow and shrubbery were beaten down and the ground covered with blood. As there were no other tracks in the vicinity than those of the bears, they were undoubtedly the belligerents. Half a mile beyond were the marks of another struggle. At this place one of the animals had taken another direction from the other two, leaving no blood in the track. He had probably become disgusted at the conduct of his companions, and left them to fight it out between themselves. I continued on the track of the two, and before night the dogs treed one of them and I shot it through the head. Near by I found a shelter about four feet wide, and twice that length, formed by a projecting rock, under which I dragged the dead bear, and prepared to pass the night. The animal bore shocking marks of the recent encounter, his throat and forward parts being so badly lacerated that he could not have survived the winter. About dark it commenced raining, and I considered myself fortunate in having found so snug a shelter. About nine o'clock two panthers made their appearance, and finding what was perhaps their usual quarters invaded, they set up a screaming that would have sent the blood to the stoutest heart. I took my gun in one hand, my tomahawk in the other, while my dog stood near me, and I resolved, if they should attack me, to give them a warm reception. They kept up their fearful serenade until midnight, when they withdrew, and I heard no more of them. In the morning all traces of the other bears was obliterated, and I was accordingly compelled to abandon the idea of any further search for them.

I have tamed at different times four bears, but disposed of them when they were about a year old, except the one I have now in my possession. I commenced training this one when he was about a year old, at first using the lash freely, but I soon found that whipping did not subdue him, but rendered him obstinate. I then tried milder means, and soon had him completely under my control. I taught him to lead by pulling gently upon the string, offering food at the same time. He soon learned to follow whenever I pulled the string, and spoke his name. After this he would perform anything I ordered, if I could make him understand what I wished. By persuasion they may be taught almost anything that a brute can learn, but will not be driven. Sometimes however, when they understand what is required of them, and refuse to obey, it may be necessary to use the lash. When a complete mastery is once obtained over it, the bear is as easily taught as any animal I ever attempted to train. They are very irritable when touched from behind, and on one occasion as I was leading my bear through a gate, he hung back, and a person struck him behind with a stick, when he sprang forward and bit me severely in the leg. At another time, while in the house, teaching him to walk backward, he struck against a table, when he seized me by the hand. He instantly lay down and began to cry, knowing the whipping which awaited him. My bear will allow any animal to approach him, but if they should touch him behind, he resents it at once. In the months of July and August, when the weather is very warm, bears require water in which to wallow. They subsist, during the early spring, upon the worms which they find under the bark of dead trees, as well as under stones and pieces of wood. When the grass and herbage begins to sprout they feed upon that, but at this season they are always savage with hunger, and will attack any animal which affords a prospect of a meal. It is at this season that they are the most troublesome to the settlements, for if they once obtain a taste of a domestic animal they will prowl around the settlement until July, when they can find plenty of blossoms and berries, of which they are very fond. As soon as nuts ripen they feed upon them, particularly acorns, chestnuts and beechnuts.

My first serious adventure with bears was when I was about fourteen years of age. Alexander Smith and James McMullen had left my father's house to hunt, and tracked seven raccoons to their hole in the rocks. Having no means of driving them out, they returned home. The next day we prepared matches and yellow pitch pine torches, and I accompanied them. When we arrived at the hole, Smith and myself entered, while McMullen remained outside to kill them as they emerged. The entrance for twenty-five feet was high enough to admit our walking upright, when it became narrower, and we were compelled to creep upon our hands and knees. We penetrated as far as necessary, and then, throwing in a lighted match, we lay still, waiting the result. Four of the animals soon went past us, and the next moment we heard the report of Smith's gun. Upon arriving at the outside, however, we ascertained that he had not killed any of the animals, having become so much excited that he had fired at random. The next time Smith remained outside with the gun, and McMullen entered the cave with me. We went in about as far as before, threw our matches, and listened. In a short time I heard a noise that I thought was produced by some animals larger than a raccoon. I took the light from the hand of my companion, and peering into the hole I discovered two bears moving toward us. I told McMullen, who secreted himself in a hole near the entrance. In attempting to follow him, I stumbled, fell, and the bears passed over me. Smith shot the largest one as it emerged from the hole. He was a very large animal, weighing three hundred pounds. As we had no dogs, the smaller one escaped.

CHAPTER XVI.

HUNTING DEER AT DIFFERENT SEASONS.

IN the latter part of June, deer generally keep themselves in the swales, or marshes, near the small streams, where the grass starts the earliest. The usual method of hunting them at these places was to encamp in the vicinity, and watch early in the morning and late at evening, when they go out to feed. If the woods are not open, the hunter ascended a tree or eminence where he could command a more extended view. When he discovered a deer, he slipped down, and endeavored to approach it by another direction than the one in which they were moving, as they always look behind them for danger. It is always necessary for the hunter to keep on the lee-ward side of the deer, as their keen scent will detect his presence and flee, long before he can approach within shot, if the wind blows from him to the deer. The manner of curing the meat is the same as that of the elk. It is first cut from the bone in thin slices and salted in the skin. It is easily preserved, less than a pint of salt with a little saltpeter, being sufficient for a deer. When it has lain from twelve to twenty-four hours, a scaffold is built, upon which the meat is spread, and a slow fire built underneath. If the weather was stormy, the skin could be spread over the meat, and the drying still continued, the fire being gradually increased until the meat was thoroughly cured. In the mean time the hunter could continue his operations without much interruption, as the fire had no effect in frightening away the deer. When I went on a hunt, I usually carried a good supply of salt, and arranged it so that if I did not return at the end of three days a man followed me with a horse, bringing me supplies, and conveying home the venison I had taken. During all my hunts I kept a constant lookout for deer licks, and if I found none in a place favorable for deer, I made one near an unfailing spring. The manner in which I made the lick was to bore several holes in a black oak log with an augur which I always carried with me for the purpose, and into them put about three pints of salt, with a small quantity of saltpeter, and insert a plug in each hole. The wood soon becoming saturated with the salt, the deer would gnaw it. If I found a lick to which the deer at the proper season resorted, I proceeded at once to build a scaffold, in order that the deer might become accustomed to the sight of it before I made use of it. If a tree stood within three or four rods of the lick I built my scaffold upon that. If there was no tree in a favorable place, I set four crotches in the earth, lay poles across, and make a screen of bushes or bark to conceal myself from the deer. About a month after I had prepared a log, I visited it, and if the deer had found it, I built a scaffold near it. In hunting at these licks, I mounted the scaffold by a ladder which I drew up after me, and patiently awaited the approach of the deer. If none came during the day, I prepared a torch of pitch pine, sometimes adding lard or bear's grease, which I swung upon a pole reaching from the scaffold to the ground. The torch was attached to a crane of withes and bark, made to slide upon the pole, and slipped down by a cord to within three feet of the ground. As the deer came along, they would stop and stare at the light, forming an easy mark for me. When alone in these expeditions, I was always provided with two guns, a musket and a rifle. If several deer came at once within shot, I fired the musket, which was loaded with buckshot, and the deer frequently stood fixed to the spot, not knowing which way to flee, and I could kill three or four before coming down from the scaffold. Besides the light near the ground, I had another upon the scaffold, about as high as my head, and when firing from the scaffold, I raised the gun above the range of the deer, and lower it gradually until the end of the barrel became dark, and then fire, scarcely ever missing my aim. When I fired from the ground by torchlight, I pointed the gun below the game, and raised it till the end became dark. After killing the first ones, there is no further chance that night, as the smell of the blood will frighten away the deer. I generally had a companion and a dog, and one of us remained at a distance with the dog, while the other watched from the scaffold. In the morning, if any were wounded, we set the dog on the track, if we could not track it by the blood without difficulty. About the tenth of November, the deer begin to travel from one place to another, and by that time I had generally chosen my hunting ground. I would take my station upon the summit of some hill, where I could command a view in all directions. I would some times mount a tree to the height of fifty feet. On one occasion I discovered from the top of a tree seven deer and three bears. I descended and killed two of the deer, but the bears escaped.

My first lessons in hunting were received from an old hunter, named John Mills. He lived near my father's, and wishing to remove to Canada, sold his farm to my father. He then offered to sell me his dog, and teach me all he knew about deer hunting, for fifteen dollars, which I accepted. I had already hunted several years, but his instructions were of greater value to me than all my previous experience. The substance of his instructions I have given the reader. The following autumn I went out on a hunting expedition, taking with me the dog I had bought of Mills and another one which I had previously owned. I followed the directions I had received, and with a success which showed their value. From the early part of October until the first of February I killed twenty-eight bears and a large number of deer. Mills also taught me, among other things, how to train dogs for hunting, as well as the kind of animals to select. The usual resorts for deer at different seasons, which I also learned from my Mentor are as follows. In June they frequent beech and maple woods, or feed in the marshes bordering on the streams. About the last of July they take to the highlands, among the chestnut and white oak woods, feeding on pea-vines and other herbage. In the hot weather of August they lie in the thickest shades upon high hills, and at this time the manner of hunting them is to watch by a spring, as near the summit of a hill as may be found. They will come at evening to drink, and fall an easy prey to the hunter as he lies concealed within a few yards. The last of September the deer begin to leave the thickets and move from one place to another, and for several months they are constantly in motion. The hunter has only to station himself near one of their paths, and shoot them as they pass. When the first snows come they can be tracked to the places where herds of them lie at night, and the hunter can keep near a herd and pick them off with his rifle.

In 1805 a colony consisting of about forty families of English people, made a settlement between the first and second forks of Pine Creek. They cleared about two hundred and fifty acres of land, and built several good houses, but being unaccustomed to the hardships and dangers of pioneer life, they abandoned the settlement after struggling along for five years. As soon as the coast was clear, the deer from all the country around came to feed in the cultivated fields and sunny pastures of the deserted settlement. This afforded a capital opportunity for hunters, and the place became a favorite resort for them. We would lodge in the upper story of some deserted house, and in the morning looking out of a window, could see perhaps forty deer. I have often shot a couple of deer from the window before leaving the house in the morning. From this congregation of deer in the openings a man in the vicinity conceived the idea of entrapping them in fields cleared and sowed with wheat or grass. The next season he accordingly cleared two acres, partly on a hill-side, built a high fence around it and sowed it with wheat. About the last of August, when the young wheat had obtained a good start, he made openings in the fence to admit the deer. When they had fed upon the wheat for three weeks, it was gnawed so close that he closed the fence for a few weeks to give it a fresh start. About the first of October he again opened the fence for a week, when he kept it closed till near the middle of November. The deer had now become wonted to the place, and he made places in the fence where they could easily leap into the field, but once in they could not get out. In a few days he had two bucks and two does in his enclosure. He killed the bucks, and let the does stay in the field to decoy other deer. This had the desired effect, and during the season he took in this manner between sixty and seventy deer. This method is successful only where deer are numerous. The wheat crop is not materially injured, if the deer are not permitted to remain on it too long. The best kind of dog for hunting deer is a large variety, half bloodhound, a quarter cur and the other quarter grayhound. I have had two dogs of this kind, for one of which I paid ten dollars and for the other six. They were of more practical value than four smaller dogs would have been. When they were once in chase of a deer, they would not lose one in ten. So famous did they become for their prowess, that if any of the neighbors saw them running, they would exclaim, "There are Tome's dogs; the deer cannot be far off." The deer could never baffle them by any of their usual stratagems, and they often ran them down before they reached the water. Those

wishing to hunt successfully should always procure at any
cost, the largest and best dogs to be found.

A fawn when very young, can be easily tamed and kept
near the house. They soon become attached to their home,
and if removed twenty miles will find their way back in a
few days, unless forcibly prevented. I have never succeeded
in making a deer stand and suffer me to milk her, nor in
breaking one to the halter. They can be coaxed to follow,
but will not be led. A doe, if at perfect liberty, will remain about half the time near the house where it was brought
up, and the other half in the woods, but never forgets to
return. When returning home, it always takes a straight
course, through fields, streams and forests, unless attacked.
They are very quiet and good-natured in a domesticated state,
unless they have young, and then they will stamp, kick and
drive every other animal from them. The bucks, until they
are a year old, are very mild and gentle, but even then they
will not learn to do any labor. At two years old they are
very untractable, and cannot be subdued by whipping or
any other means, but will plunge at their keeper upon every
opportunity. At three years old it is dangerous to approach
them at any time after the middle of September, when their
antlers have attained their full size, until they shed them
in February. Their viciousness increases with their years,
and unless kept in a park they are very dangerous animals.

The color of the deer changes twice during the year. They
shed their hair the last of April, and in May their color is
a bright red. By the last of October they are covered with
a short coat of a blue color. The color of the young fawns
is a light reddish-brown, beautifully variegated with small
white spots. About the middle of October these spots disappear, and they are then bluish, like the old ones. In November their hind quarters become white in places. I have
seen in my life, two white deer. The first one I saw with
a drove of other deer eating moss in the Susquehannah river,
where I was fire-hunting. Three years afterward, I saw
another, while hunting for elk at night, fifteen miles above
the place where I had seen the first. I could have killed
both, but being such rare specimens, I let them go. They
are not a distinct species of deer, but are merely deviations
from the general color of common deer. Every seventh year
in April, they move west in herds of from three to fifteen,
generally going about thirty miles from their usual haunts,
and remaining, if undisturbed until some time in July. If

they are molested, they return at once to their old haunts. This disposition to fly in danger to their accustomed place, is always shown by them, whether in a wild or domesticated state. I knew a tame buck to disappear from its owner, and nothing was heard of it for some time. At length it returned one night, very weary, but with its bell on, just as when it went away. It had taken up its quarters at a farm fifteen miles distant, where it remained contented until attacked by dogs. From the last of June until September, deer are light and in good condition for running, and at this season they are not easily run down. When driven to the water by dogs at this time they will cross and run a long time on the opposite side. By the last of October they are very fat, taking immediately to the water when pursued, and do not cross it, but run either up or down a mile or two, so that the dogs lose their scent, and then leaving the water lie down at a short distance, keeping a keen watch for their pursuers. I always found it desirable to have a man and dog at the water to watch for the deer, and with a good dog they seldom escaped. A deer will not mate with any other animal than one of its own species. If one is placed when young, in company with a calf, lamb, or any other animal, it will not, as might be expected, form an attachment for it. The bucks are very quarrelsome, and during the running season desperate conflicts often ensue between them, resulting sometimes in the death of both belligerents. I have often found two of them lying dead, at the season I have mentioned, each bearing fatal marks of the other's antlers. I once found one lying in the last gasp, his antlers interlocked with those of another, already dead. A neighbor once found two of them fighting with their antlers locked, and a doe standing near. He first shot the doe and then both bucks.

CHAPTER XVII.

NATURE AND HABITS OF THE PANTHER, WOLF AND FOX.

THE jaguar, American panther, or as it is usually corrupted by hunters, " painter " — is one of the most formidable animals encountered in the forests of this continent. It belongs to the cat tribe, and in its manner of springing upon its prey, as well as in many other particulars, it resembles the domestic cat. Its color is the same as the deer, changing in May with its new coat to a red, which changes again to a bluish color in October. They subsist entirely upon animal food, their usual prey being deer and rabbits. About the first of January, is called the running season, being the time when they mate. When the first snows of winter come, they seek the rocky hills and sheltered places, where they remain until driven forth by hunger, when they frequently visit the farmyards of the settlers, and help themselves to any sheep or fowl that is within their reach. From an Isrealitish antipathy to pork, or some other cause, they never attack a hog, passing by good fat ones to reach other animals. A half-grown panther once entered a poultry-house at night, making such a disturbance that it was heard in the dwelling by two females, who were the only ones at home. They supposed it was a fox, and taking a loaded gun and a torch, they went to the scene of the robbery. As they peered into the poultry-house, they perceived the animal, but still ignorant of its character they fired. The creature gave a yell that thrilled them with horror, and dropping their torch, they retreated to the house, but upon going out again, when all was silent, they found the panther lying dead. The females carefully conceal their young until they are half-grown, and so effectually do they accomplish it, that during a life time spent in the forest, I never found a nest with young in it. I once saw a panther thrust her head out of a hole in an old hollow tree, but as I had no gun or axe, I went home, and in a few days returned and cut down the tree. I found in it a snug, warm nest, which she had occupied with her young but she had seen me, and removed them to other quarters. They seldom have more than one at a time, and never more than two, which they probably rear in holes near the tops of trees. The bear is the only animal that can cope with the panther. I once witnessed an encounter between a bear and a panther. From its superior agility the panther had the advantage at first, but when the bear becme enraged by his wounds, he grasped his antagonist in his powerful paws, crushing and biting him to death almost instantly. Its gait is the same as that of a cat, treading stealthily along upon its toes, when moving at leisure, but when pursued or pursuing and it wishes to accelerate its pace, it moves in tremendous bounds, passing over the ground so rapidly as to defy pursuit, but it can maintain this movement but a short time, soon becoming fatigued and ascending a tree. When a panther is about to attack its prey, it creeps noiselessly along until within a few yards of it, when crouching flat, it pauses for a moment, with its eyes dilated, its tail quivering, and every muscle strained to its utmost tension, and then, with a sudden spring, it fastens upon its victim, which it soon dispatches with its teeth and long powerful claws. From this peculiar manner of attack, it is sometimes enabled to conquer even an elk, and I have twice found elk, which had been killed by panthers; one of them so recently that it was yet warm, and I killed the panther within a short distance. I have attacked a panther with eight dogs, for which it proved more than a match, driving them all from the field. Notwithstanding its ferocity and strength, it is little feared by hunters, and many of the marvelous tales of its attacks upon men are undoubtedly without foundation. It may be that in some instances they have been driven by hunger to attack the human species, but with that instinctive consciousness of man's superiority which every animal exhibits, they will generally avoid him if possible. I have often watched by the carcases of deer, which had been killed and partly devoured by panthers, but none ever returned for the remainder while I was near. They are less numerous than any other animal ranging the same forests, and are solitary in their habits, never herding together like wolves and many other animals.

The breeding season for wolves is in May, and at this season they are very shy, keeping themselves scattered through the woods, near the head waters of the streams, and seldom

approaching the settlement. An old she-wolf will occasionally sally forth and pick up a sheep. They generally have
three or four young at a time, and never more than seven.
The young wolves are weaned in November, when they have
attained their full size. When left by the old ones to shift
for themselves, they become nearly famished, and are more
troublesome to the settlements than at any other season.
In February, which is the running season, they collect in
large gangs, and do much mischief. They will attack a dog
or any other animal that they can master. In 1822, while
hunting on the Clarion River, my dogs were attacked by
wolves. One of them escaped, but the other, a valuable
animal, was torn in pieces. Frequent and sometimes fatal
conflicts occur among themselves, and I have several times
found dead ones which had been torn in pieces by their comrades. One night a gang of wolves passed my house, howling and screaming fearfully, and chasing a dog to the very
door. The next morning I found one of their number lying
dead, and another was found a few miles distant. In the
latter part of May they begin to chase deer, and from that
time until the following March, they subsist principally in
this manner. In the winter, when the snow is deep, with
a crust upon the surface, it is difficult for the deer to run,
and great numbers of them are destroyed by wolves. In the
spring, when it is more difficult for them to catch deer, they
live upon rabbits, frogs, fish, etc. I have often seen them
watching for fish in the Susquehannah. This river abounds
in a kind of fish called the white sucker, which lie in schools
near the shore, sunning themselves. The wolves come slyly
to the water and seize them, sometimes taking two or three
before the school escapes to deep water. When there was
no bounty on wolves, we did not kill them, as they were useful in driving in deer. Wolves never attack cattle, colts,
or hogs. They will intermix with dogs, and I once knew an
old she-wolf to come into the settlement and entice away
a number of dogs. The next summer she was seen with
six half-wolf pups. The hunter shot her, and endeavored
to capture the pups, but they made their escape. Two of
them had spots on them exactly like one of the dogs. A
slut belonging to an Indian living at the head of Kenzua
Creek, had a litter of half-wolf pups. They were larger than
common dogs, very sharp-scented, and would some times run
deer. In stormy weather wolves take shelter under rocks
and in hollow trees, which in the early spring, they also
occupy at night. They generally come to their nests about

sunset, and the hunter can shoot them as they arrive, by taking his station upon a tree or a scaffold, where they cannot scent him.

Of foxes there are three kinds, the black, the silver grey, and the red. The black fox is the largest and most valuable. It is very sly and cunning, seldom approaching within three or four miles of the settlement, and when hotly pursued, will ascend any tree that leans. I have killed foxes which I supposed to be a cross between the black and the silver grey. The silver grey is also very shy, and in size it is between the black and the red. They subsist upon squirrels, rabbits, mice and fish. The red fox is smaller and more numerous than either of the other varieties. Though they are not as shy as the other kinds, they still possess so much cunning that it is very difficult to catch them. The most successful manner of taking them is to track them to their holes when there is a light snow on the ground, and set traps covered with straw, near the entrance. The snow falling soon covered both trap and straw, when the foxes, not suspecting danger, would step into the trap and be caught. Another manner of trapping them is to set a trap in a spring which they frequent, and attach the bait to sticks which are set in the water beyond the traps, and as the fox attempts to reach it, he steps into the trap. After his visits to the farm-yards, the fox strikes a direct course for his hole, and a person by secreting himself near the path, can shoot them as they pass. They breed in the same manner as dogs, the litters numbering from three to six. They rear their young in holes which they dig in the ground. Young foxes are easily tamed, and will remain around the premises until the season for mating, when they generally go to the woods, and often remain. Red foxes generally stay near the settlements, preferring to live in white ash or chestnut woods, near water. I never saw a young black or silver-grey fox. So jealously do they avoid the haunts of man, that but little can be learned of its habits. Indeed, the black fox is so shy as well so rare, that its very existence is by some regarded as fabulous, and it undoubtedly forms the foundation for many a mystic tale which is recounted in awe-struck tones by the settler's children as they gather of a winter evening around the blazing hearth of their log-cabin. I never succeeded in running one down with hounds in the manner that red ones are caught. One which I was once after with hounds ran up a leaning tree and I shot it, but this was the only case in which I was successful with dogs.

CHAPTER XVIII.

RATTLESNAKES AND THEIR HABITS.

HAVING always lived where rattle-snakes were numerous, I have taken particular notice of their habits. It was only after ten years observation that I learned the manner in which they travel when they emerge from their holes, how they propogate, and how they live at different seasons. It is a common error to suppose that a new rattle is added every year to their tail. I had two rattle-snakes which were taken when about three years old, and both had by some accident, lost all but one of their rattles. In three months three new rattles had grown upon one and one upon the other. Rattle-snakes shed their skin in June. It first begins to loosen at the tail, and gradually approaches the head, coming off entire a day or two after it is loose at the head. About this time they collect together in large numbers, upon rocks near the water. I have seen forty of them sunning themselves upon one rock, and have heard others tell of seeing three hundred together. When they have remained at these places a few weeks, they mate and disperse. Many suppose that the black ones are males and the yellow are females. This is a mistake; as I have seen two of each color together. The ones which I owned were both males, and one was yellow and the other black. The black one was bitten by the other, from the effect of which it died in about a week. In July they lay their eggs in the sand on the margin of rivers and creeks, a little above high water mark. The eggs are about as large as those of a quail, and are all deposited at one time. They always lay an odd number, seven, nine or eleven. After leaving their eggs in the sand for about four weeks they return and swallow them. I never saw this done, but I have watched the place where the eggs were deposited, and at the end of four weeks the eggs were gone, the sand disturbed and the track of the snake could be seen. An old man named James English has told me that he had seen them swallow their eggs, and at one time about the middle of September, he saw a number of small snakes issue from the mouth of the old one, and as she moved on, they followed. I cannot vouch for the truth of this as I never witnessed any thing of the kind, but have killed snakes in September, with live young in them. In my opinion the snakes swallow the eggs when they are about to hatch, in order to preserve the young until they attain some size. From the middle of June to the middle of August, the male and female are never far apart. The female takes the lead, and the male follows within a short distance. If the female is killed at this season, her mate will always be found near her within three days: A person of my acquaintance killed a female snake which he laid upon the limb of a small tree, eight feet from the ground. In a short time its mate crawled up to the limb and remained by its side for three days. After the middle of August they disperse and retire to their holes. I do not think, as many do, that they live together in dens, during the winter, but that each one finds quarters for itself, where it remains singly, until spring. While digging for a mill-pit in January, I found a snake two feet below the surface. It appeared to be frozen, but upon taking it near the fire it soon revived. They have been found under rocks and in other places, not more than a foot from the surface. They are always found lying perfectly straight, and as it is not probable that they emerge tail first from their holes, they must dig another hole to come out of. The rattle-snake moves very slowly, sometimes consuming a month in going a mile or two to the water. They sometimes lie upon the surface of the water and float some distance. When in the water they become bloated, but soon recover their natural size, after leaving the water. Besides rattle-snakes, the country east of the Allegany mountains was infested by copperheads, blowing vipers, black-snakes, racers and hoop, or horn-snakes. The copperheads were not as numerous as the rattle-snakes, but are much more venomous and spiteful, striking at everything that comes within their reach. The blowing viper is so named from its emitting a hissing like that produced by the blowing of a goose. It is larger than the copperhead, but not as venomous, being more so however, than the rattle-snake. The black-snakes were very numerous, and so many are still found in all the northern States that every one living there is familiar with their appearance. They are harmless, but very voracious, using their powers of fascination to secure birds, squirrels

[115]

and other small animals, which they afterward devour. The racer is very log and slim, sometimes growing to the length of eleven feet, while its diameter does not exceed an inch. Their color is black, with the exception of white rings around the neck. They glide over the ground with their heads elevated about eighteen inches, as rapidly as a dog can run. I was at one time while plowing, very much alarmed by one of these snakes. I heard a hissing, but passed on without paying much regard to it. When I again came around to the place, it was repeated, but I passed on as before. When I approached the spot the third time my curiosity was excited, and I resolved to ascertain the source of the hissing. When I was near the spot from which it seemed to proceed my attention was called for a moment to my team, and when I again turned my head, I was in contact with a racer, eleven feet in length, standing nearly erect, and darting his forked tongue, not more than a foot from my head. I sprang back with a scream which startled one of the horses, and plunging forward, it threw the other, broke loose, and run to the house. Recovering myself, I advanced toward the snake, when it settled down, and retreated to the hollow in which it was first concealed. I halted at a little distance, when it again raised its head erect, and stood eyeing me. As I turned to run, the snake followed me, but retreated when I advanced toward it. In this manner we chased each other alternately across the field three times, when I picked up a club and killed it. The hoop-snake, or horn-snake is very rare. It is about five feet long, and an inch and a quarter in thickness. It is similar in color to a yellow rattlesnake, but the light spots are less dingy. Its tail terminates in a black horn, four or five inches in length, and very sharp at the point. When preparing to make an attack, it bends itself into a circular form, and rolls over the ground like a hoop, striking its spike with great force into the object of its attack. So deadly is the venom contained in this spike or horn, that it is fatal even to trees. In one instance with which I was cognizant, one of these snakes rolled at a man, who avoided it, by stepping to one side, and the snake, being under such velocity that it could not turn, struck its horn into an elm tree with such force that it could not extricate it. The snake died, hanging there, in two weeks, and the tree was lifeless at the end of a month. Notwithstanding the deadly nature of a rattle-snake's bite, they are easily destroyed by dogs which have been taught how to attack them. The dog seizes it by the middle, and with a few vigorous shakes scatters it in fragments. If the dog should be bitten, it immediately digs a hole in the ground, in which it lies until the swelling disappears. I have always found this simple remedy the best one which can be resorted to for the bite of a rattle-snake. A young man of my acquaintance was once bitten, and I immediately dug a hole in the ground, eighteen inches deep, into which the leg was placed and covered with earth. At first he experienced no pain, but in a short time it became so severe that I was compelled to hold him down, but in three hours he fell asleep. After sleeping two hours he awoke, and the leg was entirely free from pain. Upon removing it from the earth, it was very white, and the poison was all drawn out. Another remedy is a plant called rattle-snake-weed or ox-wood. It is found upon low land, growing three or four feet high, with a slender stem, and limbs like those of a sun-flower. Its blossoms also resemble the sun-flower in form, but are much smaller. The juice is pressed from the leaves, and applied to the wound, as well as administered internally. In the year 1804, a man named John English was bitten by a rattle-snake while harvesting. He was struck in the large vein of the ankle, and in fifteen minutes the effects of the bite were visible in every part of his body and face. We carried him to the house, and as soon as possible obtained the weed, all of which required about half an hour. At this time his jaws were set so firmly that we were compelled to pry them open to administer the juice. He revived immediately, and we made a decoction of the weed, which we continued to give him. In four days he was able to sit up, but it was some time before he entirely recovered. A poultice of red onions, salt and gunpowder, applied to the wound, and renewed frequently, is also an effectual remedy. Before I was twenty-six years of age I had seen thousands of rattle-snakes, but had never witnessed an exhibition of the powers of fascination which they are said to possess, and was therefore incredulous upon that point. A man in my employ told me that he had seen it, but I could not be convinced until I had occular evidence. One morning in August, about the period I have mentioned, I saw a rattle-snake upon the ground, with its keen eyes fixed upon a rat, which was about eighteen inches distant, and advancing slowly toward the snake. In a few minutes it had approached close to the snake, and just as the latter was about to seize it, I struck the rat lifeless with a stick which I held in my hand. The snake instantly coiled himself and

prepared to strike at me, when I held out the stick, and he
bit it with more venom that I ever saw exhibited. He drove
his fangs in with such force that I could feel the jar of the
stick in my hand. A blow from the stick immediately placed
him where he would never charm another rat. At another
time I saw a rattle-snake charming a large black squirrel. As
soon as the animal came within reach, the snake seized it,
but the squirrel, after dragging it about twice its length,
escaped. I have also seen black-snakes climb trees and charm
birds. I have heard many say that snakes of different kinds
will mate together, but from many experiments which I have
made I am convinced that this is an error. I once saw a
rattle-snake lying upon a rock beside the water, and finding
a water-snake at a short distance, I laid it upon the rock,
near the other. It instantly fled from the rattle-snake, and
continued to, as often as I placed them near each other. At
another time I placed a black-snake near a rattle-snake, and at
first the latter took no notice of the other, which exhibited
the greatest terror, but upon placing them together again,
the rattle-snake flew at it and would have bitten it, had it
not been too nimble, and eluded the stroke. The rage of the
one and the terror of the other increased, as I continued to
place them near each other. When a rattle-snake and a
blowing-viper were brought together, both ran, each seem-
ing to have an instinctive dread of the other. Finding a copperhead and a blowing-viper at the same time, I brought them
together, when the viper beat a retreat, but the copperhead
made no attempt to bite it. The last experiment I made was
to place together a water-snake and an eel. Contrary to
what might have been expected, the snake ran from the eel.
These experiments convinced me that there is no affinity
between snakes of different kinds, but that those which are
less venomous are kept in terror by those which are more so.
I have generally found snakes very numerous south of the
New York State line, between Tioga river and Lake Erie.
They were always very numerous east of the Allegany mountains, but the State of New York was never as badly infested
with them as Pennsylvania. I have endeavored, in a former
chapter, to give some idea of their numbers in the country
lying upon Pine Creek. West of there, upon the Sinemahoning it was little better in this respect, but from there
to the Allegany river, the country was clear of them. They
were very numerous on both sides of this river, but were not
as troublesome north of the State line as they were nearer
its mouth.

CHAPTER XIX.

DISTINGUISHED LUMBERMEN, ETC.

LUMBER is the great staple of trade in this section of country, and among those most prominent in this business, none stand higher than GUY C. IRVIN. He has been justly called the Napoleon of the lumber business. His name, person, and character are known in every large town from Olean to New Orleans. Coming into the section at an early day with little capital save a vigorous and comprehensive mind and an untiring spirit of enterprise, he has amassed a large fortune, having owned more pine timber lands and sawmills than any other individual upon the Allegany. When the business was driven to its extent in 1836-38, he frequently sent to market twenty million feet of lumber in a single season, and both shores for a mile above Pittsburgh are sometimes lined with his rafts, waiting a rise of the water. I have been acquainted with him from childhood, and it is in the hope that young men will follow the example thus held up to them, that I record his character and career. In his business operations he never loses sight of the rights or welfare of the laboring classes. I never knew him, upon any pretext, to pay those running his lumber less than was agreed upon, but on the contrary he has often made up, out of his own purse, for the mishaps of those in his employ. Upon one occasion he advanced seven hundred dollars more than had been agreed upon for running two million feet of boards to Louisville. He never hoards his money, but keeps it constantly in circulation, building mills, sawing and buying lumber and running it from the head waters of the Allegany to points on the Ohio and to New Orleans. He built a flouring mill on the Connewango, seven miles from Warren. At the same place he also built a gang sawmill, several single sawmills, and a railroad for conveying his timber, together with the mansion where he resides, which is the most elegant and commodious residence in the county. Besides these, the aggregate cost of which could not have been less than thirty thousand dollars, he has built a flouring mill at Kennedyville, costing four thousand dollars, and two double sawmills nine miles below Olean. He was also a partner with Henry Saxton, in building on the Indian Reservation a mill costing between eight and ten thousand dollars, and a mill above the State line, on the Allegany river, which cost some ten thousand dollars. When his contracts have expired, the money is always ready, and he has often advanced it before, when he thought the work was progressing properly. I was once present at Louisville when he settled with his men for running eighteen million feet of lumber, two millions of it having been rafted by me. I received a dollar and seventy-five cents per thousand, and some of the others two dollars. There were also five or six millions of shingles, for running which he paid thirty-one and a half cents per thousand. This large amount was not only paid in full, but some who had met with ill success and had still done their duty faithfully were paid more than had been agreed upon. I once made a contract to raft lumber for him, and three months before I commenced operations he asked me if I wished any advance of funds. I answered that I had done nothing yet, and could not expect any advance, but upon his repeating the offer I told him that if he was willing I would be glad to have him advance sufficient to purchase provisions while I was rafting. He handed me nearly two hundred dollars, which proved very acceptable. I saw him next at Bucktooth mills, where he came to see how I was progressing. He again offered to advance funds if I desired it. I told him I would like fifty dollars, as I wished to be prepared to pay off and discharge any hand that proved incompetent. He gave me two hundred and fifty dollars, asking me if that would be sufficient. I have run seven million feet of boards for him in 3 successive years, and while engaged I never wanted money without obtaining it. One season having met with bad luck, he presented me with a hundred dollars. The secret of his success I consider to be his punctuality in his business engagements; always doing as he agreed, so that the most implicit reliance could be placed upon his word. I think he possesses more tact in selling his lumber readily and obtaining good prices than any other lumberman I ever knew. His mansion is always open to every one, and his urbanity and affability is the same to rich and poor. No word of censure was ever breathed against him until the failure of the Lumberman's Bank at Warren, when for a short time reports injurious to his reputation were circulated, but he outlived them, and was almost the only one who paid his indebtedness to the Bank. Whenever a transaction terminates to his satisfaction he is always willing to share his good fortune with others, who have aided in bringing it about. At one time while I was interpreter for the Seneca chiefs, I acted in that capacity for them in negotiating with a number of persons, one of whom was Mr. Irvin, for a lease of land on which to build mills. It required two days to complete the arrangements, during which time my whole efforts were exerted for the benefit of the Indians, but before going away, Mr. Irvin gave me twenty-five dollars in cash, and said that I had done so well for the Indians, I might have twenty-five thousand feet of boards at the Bucktooth Mills, worth at that time fifty dollars, saying that if I had not earned it then he was sure I would some other time.

Mr. Irvin, in company with Edwin Sanderson and Mr. Clark, of Vermont, are now erecting on Willow Creek, in McKean county, the most extensive sawmill in that section of country, to be driven by steam, in addition to two good mills they now have, driven by water power. They are the owners of about seventeen thousand acres of excellent land, covered with pine, hemlock, maple, beech, chestnut and oak. They are also building a plank road four miles in length, from their mills to the river. They paid in cash for their land, over seventy thousand dollars, and are paying cash for every thing they require in building, thereby doing great good to the inhabitants of the neighborhood — more than any other establishment on the Allegany. They have also built a number of dwelling-houses and barns. The steam mill is expected to saw about thirty-five thousand feet of lumber per hour. They intend building this year a railroad through their land, which, with buildings to be erected, will furnish employment for a large number of persons. The lands of these gentlemen still abound with bears and deer, furnishing fine ground for the hunter. Corydon, at the mouth of Willow Creek, is a flourishing village, chiefly owing to the enterprise of the gentlemen above-named.

Dr. William Irwin, who resides at the mouth of Brokenstraw creek, is considered the wealthiest man in Warren county. He owns a very large tract of fine land at the mouth of the creek, a valuable grist-mill, a large double saw-mill, a woolen factory, an iron foundry, the Cornplanter Hotel, a store and a large tract of pine timber land, up the Broken-straw, upon which are four or five stone dwellings. In addition to the above, he is the owner of more than one hundred thousand acres of land in different parts of the country, on which are many mills, stores and houses. His wife was a most exemplary woman, devoting her whole life to deeds of benevolence. Her active charity did not stop with feeding and clothing all the destitute within her reach, but she was mindful of their spiritual wants, and opened a Sabbath School in her own house, bringing in all in the vicinity. Among her other good deeds she built at a cost of four thousand dollars, a stone church for the Presbyterian congregation of which she was a member. Her earthly labors ended soon after its completion, the first sermon ever preached in it being upon the occasion of her funeral, and her remains were the first laid in the adjoining graveyard. She was universally lamented, and will long live in the memory of those who knew her, as one of those upon whom the bestowal of wealth is a blessing to all within their influence.

CHAPTER XX

FEW names are more distinguished in the frontier history of Penna. than that of Cornplanter. His Indian name was Ganiodieuh, or handsome Lake. He was born at Conewangus, on the Genesee River, being a half-breed, the son of a white man named John O'Bail, a trader from the Mohawk valley. In a letter written in later years to the Governor of Pennsylvania, he thus speaks of his early youth: "When I was a child I played with the butterfly, the grasshopper and the frogs; and as I grew up I began to pay some attention and play with the Indian boys in the neighborhood; and they took notice of my skin being of a different color from theirs, and spoke about it. I inquired of my mother the cause, and she told me that my father was a resident of Albany. I still ate my victuals out of a bark dish. I grew up to be a young man, and married me a wife, and I had no kettle or gun. I then knew where my father lived, and went to see him, and found he was a white man, and spoke the English language. He gave me victuals while I was at his house, but when I started to return home, he gave me no provisions to eat on the way. He gave me neither kettle nor gun. * * *" Little further is known of his early life, beyond the fact that he was allied with the French in the engagement against Braddock, in July, 1775. He was probably at that time about seventeen years old. During the Revolution he was a war chief of high rank, in the full vigor of manhood, active, sagacious, eloquent and brave; and he most probably participated in the principal engagements against the United States, during that war. He is supposed to have been present at the cruelties of Wyoming and Cherry Valley, in which the Senecas took a prominent part. He was in the war-path with Brant during Gen. Sullivan's campaign, in 1779, and in the following year under Brant and Sir John Johnson, he led the Senecas in sweeping through Schoharie

Kill and the Mohawk. On this occasion he took his father prisoner, but with such caution as to avoid an immediate recognition. After marching the old man ten or twelve miles, he stepped before him, faced about and addressed him in the following terms:

"My name is John O'Bail, commonly called Cornplanter. I am your son! You are my father! You are my prisoner, and subject to the rules of Indian warfare. But you shall not be harmed. You need not fear. I am a warrior! Many are the scalps I have taken! Many prisoners I have tortured to death! I am your son. I was anxious to see you, and greet you in friendship. I went to your cabin and took you by force, but your life shall be spared. Indians love their friends and their kindred, and treat them with kindness. If now you choose to follow the fortunes of your yellow son, and live with our people, I will cherish your old age with plenty of venison, and you shall live easy. But if it is your choice to return to your fields and live with your white children, I will send a party of my trusty young men to conduct you back in safety. I respect you, my father. You have been friendly to Indians, and they are your friends." The elder O'Bail preferred his white children and green fields to his yellow offspring and the wild woods, and chose to return. Notwithstanding his bitter hostility while the war continued, Cornplanter became the fast friend of the United States, when once the hatchet was buried. His sagacious intellect comprehended at a glance the growing power of the States, and the abandonment with which Great Britain had requited the fidelity of the Senecas. He therefore threw all his influence at the treaties of Fort Stanwix and Fort Harmer in favor of peace; and notwithstanding the vast concessions which he saw his people were necessitated to make, still, by his energy and prudence in the negotiation, he retained for them an ample and beautiful reservation. For the course which he pursued on those occasions, the State of Pennsylvania granted him the fine reservation upon which he resided, on the Allegany river. The Senecas, however, were never well satisfied with his course in relation to these treaties; and Red Jacket, more artful and eloquent than his elder rival, but less frank and honest, seized upon this circumstance to promote his own popularity at the expense of Cornplanter. Having buried the hatchet, Cornplanter sought to make his talents useful to his people by conciliating the good will of the whites, and securing from further encroachment the little remnant of the national domain. On more than one occasion, when some reckless and bloodthirsty whites on the frontier had massacred unoffending Indians in cold blood, did Cornplanter interfere to restrain the vengeance of his people. During all the Indian wars from 1791 to 1794, which terminated with Wayne's treaty, Cornplanter pledged himself that the Senecas should remain friendly to the States. He often gave notice to the garrison at Fort Franklin of intended attacks from hostile parties and even hazarded his life on a mediatorial mission to the Western Tribes. He ever entertained a high respect and personal friendship for Washington, "the great counsellor of the thirteen fires," and often visited him during his presidency, on the business of his tribe. His speeches on these occasions exhibit both his talent in composition, and his adroitness in diplomacy. Washington fully reciprocated his respect and friendship. They had fought against each other on the disastrous day of Braddock's defeat. Both were then young men. More than forty years afterward, when Washington was about retiring from the presidency, Cornplanter made a special visit to Philadelphia to take an affectionate leave of the great benefactor of both the white and the red man. After peace was permanently established between the Indians and the United States, Cornplanter retired from public life, and devoted his labors to his own people. He deplored the evils of intemperance and exerted himself to suppress them. The benevolent efforts of missionaries among his tribe always received his encouragement, and at one time his own heart seemed to be softened by the words of truth; yet he preserved in his later years many of the peculiar notions of the Indian faith. In the war of 1812-14, when the Senecas took up the hatchet in alliance with the United States, Cornplanter appears to have taken no active part; but his son, Major Henry O'Bail and his intimate friend and neighbor, Halftown, were conspicuous in several engagements on the Niagara frontier. Rev. Timothy Alden, President of Allegany College, who visited Cornplanter in 1816, thus describes the aged chief:

"Jennesadaga, or Brant Town, Cornplanter's village, is on a handsome piece of bottom land, and comprises about a dozen dwellings. It was grateful to notice the agricultural habits of the place, and the numerous enclosures of buckwheat, corn and oats. We also saw a number of oxen, cows and horses, and many logs designed for the sawmill and the

Pittsburg market. In the year 1815, the Western Missionary Society established a school in the village under Mr. Samuel Oldham. Cornplanter, as soon as apprised of our arrival, came over to see us, and took charge of our horses. Though having many around him to obey his commands, yet in the ancient patriarchal style, he chose to serve us himself, and actually went into the field, cut the oats, and fed our beasts. He appears to be about sixty-eight years of age, five feet ten inches in height. His countenance is strongly marked with intelligence and reflection. Contrary to the aboriginal custom, his chin is covered with a beard three or four inches in length. His house is of princely dimensions, compared with most Indian huts, and has a piazza in front. He is the owner of thirteen hundred acres of excellent land, six hundred of which encircle the ground plot of his little town. He receives an annual stipend from the United States, of two hundred and fifty dollars. Cornplanter's brother, lately deceased, called the Prophet, was known by the high-sounding name of Goskakewanna Konnediu, or Large Beautiful Lake. Kinjuquade, the name of another chief, signified "The Place of Many Fishes," hence, probably, the name of Kenzua.

In 1821-22, the Commissioners of Warren county assumed the right to tax the private property of Cornplanter, and proceeded to enforce its collection. The old chief resisted, conceiving it not only unlawful, but a personal indignity. The sheriff again appeared with a small posse of armed men. Cornplanter took the deputation to a room around which were ranged about a hundred rifles, and with the sentious brevity of an Indian, intimated that for each rifle a warrior would appear at his call. The sheriff and his men withdrew, determined to call out the militia. Several prudent citizens, fearing a sanguinary collision, sent for the old chief in a friendly way, to come to Warren and compromise the matter. He came, and after some persuasion, gave his note for the tax, amounting to $43.79. He addressed, however, a remonstrance to the Governor of Pennsylvania, soliciting a return of his money, and an exemption from such demands against land which the state itself had presented to him. The Legislature annulled the tax and sent two Commissioners to explain the matter to him. He met them at the court-house in Warren, on which occasion he delivered the following speech, eminently characteristic of himself and his race:

"Brothers: Yesterday was appointed for us all to meet here. The talk which the Governor sent us pleased us very much. I think that the Great Spirit is very much pleased, that the white people have been induced so as to assist the Indians as they have done, and that he is pleased also to see the great men of this State and of the United States so friendly to us. We are much pleased with what has been done." * * * "The Great Spirit first made the world, and next the flying animals, and found all things good and prosperous. He is immortal and everlasting. After finishing the flying animals he came down on earth and there stood. Then he made different kinds of trees, and weeds of all sorts, and people of every kind. He made the spring and other seasons, and the weather suitable for planting. These he did make. But stills to make whiskey to be given to the Indians he did not make. The Great Spirit bids me tell the white people not to give the Indians this kind of liquor. When the Great Spirit had made the earth and its animals, he went into the great lakes, where he breathed as easily as any where else, and then made all the different kinds of fish. The Great Spirit looked back on all that he had made. The different kinds he made to be separate, not to mix with and disturb each other. But the white people have broken his command, by mixing their color with the Indians. The Indians have done better by not doing so. The Great Spirit wishes that all wars and fightings would cease. He next told us that there were three things for our people to attend to: first, we ought to take care of our wives and children; secondly, the white people ought to attend to their farms and cattle; thirdly, the Great Spirit has given the bears and deer to the Indians. He is the cause of all things that exist, and it is very wicked to go against his will. The Great Spirit wishes me to inform the people that they should quit drinking intoxicating drink, as being the cause of disease and death. He told us never to sell any more of our lands, for he never sold lands to any one. Some of us now keep the seventh day, but I wish to quit it, for the Great Spirit made it for others but not for the Indians, who ought every day to attend to their business. He has ordered me to quit intoxicating drink, and not to lust after any woman but my own, and informs me that by so doing I should live the longer. He has made known to me that it is very wicked to tell lies. Let no one suppose this I have said is not true." * * * "I have now to thank the Governor for what he has done. I have informed him what the Great Spirit has ordered me to cease from, and I wish the Governor to

inform others of what I have communicated. This is all
I have at present to say."

The old chief appears after this again to have fallen into
seclusion, taking no part even in the politics of his people.
He died at his residence, on the 7th of March, 1836, at the
age of one hundred and upward. "Whether at the time of
his death he expected to go to the fair hunting grounds of
his own people, or to the heaven of the Christian, is not
known." "Notwithstanding his professional Christianity,
Cornplanter was very superstitious. 'Not long since,' says
Mr. Foote, of Chautauque county, 'he said the Good Spirit
had told him not to have any thing to do with the white
people, or even to preserve any mementoes or relics that had
been given him, from time to time, by the pale-faces —
whereupon, among other things, he burnt up his belt, and
broke his elegant sword." In reference to the personal appearance of Cornplanter at the close of his life, a writer
in the *Democratic Arch*, (Venango county,) says: "I once
saw the aged and venerable chief and had an interesting in-
terview with him, about a year and a half before his death.
I thought of many things, when seated near him, beneath
the wide-spreading shade of an old sycamore, on the banks of
the Allegany — many things to ask him — the scenes of the
Revolution, the generals that fought its battles and conquered the Indians, his tribe, the Six nations, and himself.
He was constitutionally sedate, was never observed to smile,
much less to indulge in the 'luxury of a laugh.' When I
saw him he estimated his age to be over one hundred years.
I think one hundred and three was about his reckoning of
it. This would make him near one hundred and five years
old at the time of his decease. His person was much stooped,
and his stature was far short of what it had once been —
not being over five feet six inches, at the time I speak of.
Mr. John Strathers of Ohio, told me some years since, that
he had seen him nearly fifty years ago, and at that period
he was about his own height, viz: six feet one inch. Time
and hardship had made dreadful impressions upon that ancient
form. The chest was sunken and his shoulders were drawn
forward, making the upper part of his body resemble a
trough. His feet, too, (for he had to take off his moccasins,)
were deformed and haggard by injury. I would say that
most of the fingers on one hand were useless; the sinews
had been severed by a blow of the tomahawk or scalping
knife. How I longed to ask him what scene of blood and

strife had thus stamped the enduring evidence of its existence upon his person! But to have done so would, in all probability, have put an end to all further conversation on any subject — the information desired would certainly not have been obtained — and I had to forego my curiosity. He had but one eye, and even the socket of the lost organ was hidden by the overhanging brow resting upon the high cheek bone. His remaining eye was of the brightest and blackest hue. Never have I seen one, in young or old, that equalled it in brilliancy. Perhaps it had borrowed luster from the eternal darkness of its neighboring orbit. His ears had been dressed in the Indian mode: all but the outside ring had been cut away. On one ear this ring had been torn asunder near the top, and hung down his neck like a useless rag. He had a full head of hair, white as the driven snow, which covered a head of ample dimensions and admirable shape. His face was swarthy; but this may be accounted for from the fact that he was but half-Indian. He told me that he had been at Franklin more than eighty years before the period of our conversation, on his passage down the Mississippi, with the warriors of his tribe, on some expedition against the Creeks or Osages. He had long been a man of peace, and I believe his great characteristics were humanity and truth. It is said that Brant and Cornplanter were never friends after the massacre of Cherry Valley. Some have alleged, because the Wyoming massacre was perpetrated by the Senecas, that Cornplanter was there. Of the justice of this suspicion there are many reasons for doubt. It is certain that he was not the chief of the Senecas at this time; the name of the chief in that expedition was Ge-en-quah-toh, or He-goes-in-the-Smoke. As he stood before me — the aged chief in ruins — how forcibly was I struck with the truth of the beautiful figure of the old aboriginal chieftain, who, in describing himself, said he was ' like an aged hemlock, dead at the top, and whose branches alone were green.' After more than a hundred years of most varied life — of strife — of danger — of peace — he at last slumbers in deep repose on the banks of his own beloved Allegany." — [From Sherman Day's *Historical Collections of the State of Pennsylvania*.]

CHAPTER XXI.

INDIAN ELOQUENCE.

THEIR natural eloquence is acknowledged by every person who has heard their orators speak. In order, therefore, that the reader may be convinced of this, I shall offer a few specimens, the authors of some of which were personal acquaintances of my own:

SPEECH OF CORNPLANTER.

(The Speech of Cornplanter to President Washington, at Philadelphia, in the year 1790).

Father: the voice of the Seneca nation speaks to you, the great counsellor, in whose heart the wise men of all the thirteen fires have placed their wisdom. It may be very small in your ears, and we therefore entreat you to hearken with attention; for we are able to speak of things which to us are very great.

When your army entered the country of the Six Nations, we called you the Town Destroyer; to this day, when this name is heard, our women look behind and turn pale, and our children cling close to the necks of their mothers.

When our chiefs returned from Fort Stanwix and laid before our council what had been done there, our nation was surprised to hear how great a country you had compelled them to give up to you, without paying to us anything for it; every one said that your hearts were yet swelled with resentment against us for what had happened during the war, but that one day you would consider it with more kindness. We asked each other, What have we done to deserve such severe chastisement?

Father: when you kindled your thirteen fires separately, the wise men assembled at them told us you were all brothers; the children of one great father, who regarded the red people as his children. They called us brothers, and invited us to his protection. They told us that he resided beyond the great water, where the sun first rises; and that he was a king whose power no people could resist, and that his goodness was as bright as the sun. What they said went to our hearts; we accepted the invitation and promised to obey him. What the Seneca nation promise they faithfully perform. When you refused obedience to that king, he commanded us to assist his beloved men in making you sober. In obeying him we did no more than yourselves had led us to promsie.

We were deceived; but your people teaching us to confide in that king, had helped to deceive us; and we now appeal to your heart. Is all the blame ours?

Father: when we saw that we had been deceived, and heard the invitation which you gave us to draw near to the fire you had kindled, and talk with you concerning peace, we made haste toward it: you told us you could crush us to nothing; and you demanded from us a great country, as the price of that peace which you had offered to us, as if our want of strength had destroyed our rights. Our chiefs had felt your power and were unable to contend against you, and they therefore gave up that country. What they agreed has bound our nation, but your anger against us must by this time be cooled, and although our strength has not increased, nor your power become less, we ask you to consider calmly — Were the terms dictated to us by your commissioners reasonable and just?

SPEECH OF RED JACKET TO A MISSIONARY.

Friend and brother, it was the will of the Great Spirit that we should meet together this day. He orders all things, and he has given us a fine day for our council. He has taken this garment from the sun and caused it to shine with brightness on us. Our eyes are opened, that we see clearly: our ears unstopped, that we have been able to hear distinctly the words that you have spoken; for all these favors we thank the Great Spirit and him only.

Brother, this council fire was kindled by you; it was at your request that we came together at this time; we have listened with attention to what you have said; you requested us to speak our minds freely; this gives us great joy, for we now consider that we stand upright before you, and can speak what we think, all have heard your voice, and all speak to you as one man; our minds are agreed.

Brother, you say you want an answer to your talk before
you leave this place. It is right you should have one, as
you are a great distance from home, and we do not wish to
detain you; but we will first look back a little and tell you
what our fathers have told us, and what we have heard from
the white people.

Brother, listen to what we say. There was a time when
our forefathers owned this great land. Their seats extended
from the rising to the setting sun. The Great Spirit had
made it for the use of the Indians. He had created the buffalo, the deer, and other animals for food. He had made the
bear and the beaver, and their skins served us for clothing.
He had scattered them over the country, and taught us
how to take them. He had caused the earth to produce
corn for bread, and this he had done for his red children,
because he loved them. If we had any disputes about hunting grounds, they were generally settled without the shedding
of much blood; but an evil day came upon us; your forefathers crossed the great waters and landed on this island.
Their numbers were small; they found tribes, and not enemies; they told us they had fled from their own country,
for fear of wicked men, and come here to enjoy their re-
ligions. They asked for a small seat; we took pity on them
granted their request, and they sat down among us; we gave
them corn and meat; they gave us poison in return.

The white people had now found our country, tidings were
carried back, and more came among us, yet we did not fear
them, we took them to be friends; they called us brothers;
we believed them, and gave them a larger seat. At length
their numbers had greatly increased; they wanted more land;
they wanted our country. Our eyes were opened, and our
minds became uneasy. Wars took place; Indians were hired
to fight against Indians; and many of our people were destroyed. They also brought strong liquors among us; it was
strong and powerful, and has slain thousands.

Brother, our seats were once large, and yours were very
small; you have now become a great people, and we have
scarcely a place left to spread our blankets; you have got our
country, but are not satisfied; you want to force your religion upon us.

Brother, continue to listen. You say that you are sent
to instruct us how to worship the Great Spirit agreeably
to his mind, and if we do not take hold of the religion you
white people teach, we shall be unhappy hereafter; you say

that you are right, and we are lost; how do we know this to be true? We understand that your religion is written in a book; if it was intended for us as well as you, why has not the Great Spirit given it to us, and not only to us, but why did he not give to our forefathers the knowledge of that book, with the means of understanding it rightly? We only know what you tell us about it; how shall we know what to believe, being so often deceived by the white people?

Brother, you say there is but one way to worship and serve the Great Spirit; if there is but one religion, why do you white people differ so much about it? Why not agree, as you can all read the book?

Brother, we do not understand these things; we are told that your religion which was given to your forefathers, and has been handed down 'from father to son. We also have a religion which was given to our forefathers, and has been handed down to us, their children. We worship that way. It teaches us to be thankful for all the favors we receive; to love each other, and to be united. We never quarrel about our religion.

Brother, the Great Spirit has made us all; but he has made a great difference between his white and his red children; he has given us a different complexion and different customs; to you he has given the arts, to these he has not opened our eyes; we know these things to be true. Since he has made so great a difference between us in other things, why may we not conclude that he has given us a different religion according to our understanding? The Great Spirit does right, he knows what is best for his children; we are satisfied.

Brother, we do not wish to destroy your religion or take it from you; we only want to enjoy our own.

Brother, you say that you have not come to get our land or our money, but to enlighten our minds. I will now tell you that I have been at your meetings, and saw you collecting money from the meeting. I cannot tell what this money was intended for, but suppose it was for your minister, and if we should conform to your way of thinking, perhaps you may want some from us.

Brother, we have been told that you have been preaching to white people in this place; these people are our neighbors; we are acquainted with them; we will wait awhile and see what effect it has upon them.

SPEECH OF RED JACKET.

What! do you denounce us as fools and bigots, because we still continue to believe that which you sedulously inculcated two centuries ago? Your divines have thundered this doctrine from the pulpit, your judges have pronounced it from the bench, your courts of justice have sanctioned it with the formalities of law, and you would now punish our unfortunate brother (he that killed the woman) for adherance to the superstitions of his fathers! Go to Salem! Look at the records of your government, and you will find hundreds executed for the very crime which has called forth the sentence of condemnation upon this woman, and drawn down the arm of vengeance upon her. What have your brothers done more than the rulers of your people have done? and what crime has this man committed by executing, in a summary way, the laws of his nation and the injunctions of his God?

SPEECH OF BLACK HAWK, WHEN HE SURRENDERED HIMSELF TO THE AGENT AT PRAIRIE DU CHIEN.

You have taken me prisoner with all my warriors. I am much grieved, for I expected, if I did not defeat you, to hold out much longer, and give more trouble before I surrendered. I tried hard to bring you into ambush, but your last general, understands Indian fighting. I determined to rush on you, and fight you face to face; I fought hard. But your guns were well aimed. The bullets flew like birds in the air, and whizzed by our ears like the wind through the trees in winter. My warriors fell around me; it began to look dismal. I saw my evil day at hand. The sun rose dim on us in the morning, and at night it sank in a dark cloud, and looked like a ball of fire. That was the last sun that shone on Black Hawk. His heart is dead, and no longer beats quick in his bosom. He is now a prisoner to the white man; they will do with him as they wish. But he can stand torture and is not afraid of death. He is no coward. Black Hawk is an Indian. He has done nothing for which an Indian ought to be ashamed. He has fought for his countrymen, the squaws and papooses, against white men, who came, year after year, to cheat them and take away their lands. You know the cause of our making war. It is known to all white men. They ought to be ashamed of it. The white men despise the Indians, and drive them from their homes. But the Indians are not deceitful. The white men speak bad of the Indian and look at him spitefully. But the Indian does not tell lies; Indians do not steal.

An Indian who is as bad as the white men could not live in our nation; he would be put to death, and eaten up by wolves. The white men are bad school-masters; they carry false looks and deal in false actions; they smile in the face of the poor Indian to cheat him; they shake them by the hand to gain their confidence, to make them drunk, to deceive them, to ruin their wives [lives ?]. We told them to let us alone, and keep away from us; but they followed on, and beset our paths, and they coil themselves among us, like the snake. They poisoned us by their touch. We are not safe. We lived in danger. We were becoming like them, hypocrites and liars, adulterers and lazy drones, all talkers and no workers. We looked up to the Great Spirit. We went to our father. We were encouraged. His great council gave us fair words and big promises, but we got no satisfaction, things were growing worse. There were no deer in the forest. The oppossum and beaver were fled; the springs were drying up, and our squaws and pappooses without food to keep them from starving; we called a great council, and kindled a large fire. The spirit of our fathers arose and spoke to us to avenge our wrongs or die. We all spoke before the council fire. It was warm and pleasant. We set up the war whoop, and dug up the tomahawk; our knives were ready, and the heart of Black Hawk swelled high in his bosom, when he led his warriors to battle. He is satisfied. He will go to the world of spirits contented. He has done his duty. His father will meet him there, and commend him.

Black Hawk is a true Indian, and disdains to cry like a woman. He feels for his wife, his children and friends. But he does not care for himself. He cares for the nation and the Indians. They will suffer. He laments their fate. The white men do not scalp the head; but they do worse — they poison the heart; it is not pure with them. His countrymen will not be scalped, but they will, in a few years, become like the white men, so that you cannot trust them, and there must be, as in the white settlements, nearly as many officers as men, to take care of them and keep them in order.

Farewell, my nation! Black Hawk tried to save you, and avenge your wrongs. He drank the blood of some of the whites. He has been taken prisoner, and his plans are stopped. He can do no more. He is near his end. His sun is setting, and will rise no more. Farewell to Black Hawk.

RED JACKET AND THE WYANDOT CLAIM TO SUPREMACY.

At a great council of the western tribes, assembled near Detroit, prior to the late war, the celebrated Seneca orator, Red Jacket, was present, when the right of the Wyandots to light the council fire, was brought up. This claim he strenuously resisted, and administered a rebuke to this nation in the following terms:

"Have the Quatoghies forgotten themselves? Or do they suppose we have forgotten them? Who gave you the right in the west or east, to light the general council fire? You must have fallen asleep, and dreamed that the Six Nations were dead! Who permitted you to escape from the lower country? Had you any heart to speak for yourselves? Remember how you hung on by the bushes. You had not even a place to land on. You have not done p——g for fear of the Konoshioni. High claim, indeed for a tribe who had to run away from the Kadarakwa.

"As for you, my nephews," he continued, turning to the Lenapes, or Delawares, "it is fit you should let another light your fire. Before Miquon came, we had put out your fire, and put water on it; it would not burn. Could you hunt or plant without our leave? Could you sell a foot of land? Did not the voice of the Long House cry 'go!' and you went? Had you any power at all? Fit act, indeed, for you to give in to our wandering brothers — you, from whom we took the war-club and put on petticoats."

LETTER FROM REV. ASHER BLISS TO H. R. SCHOOLCRAFT.

Cattaraugus Mission, Sept. 4th, 1845.

DEAR SIR: — Agreeably to your request, I forward you some facts in regard to the establishment and progress of the gospel among the natives of this reservation. The Cattaraugus Mission Church was organized July 8th, 1827, (which is a little more than eighteen years). It consisted of Mr. William A. Thayer, the teacher, his wife and twelve native members. There have been additions to it from time to time, until the whole number who have held a connection with this church is one hundred and eighteen. Thirteen of these have been white persons, and most of them connected with the mission family. Of the one hundred and five native members, seven or eight have come by letter from other reservations, so that the number who have united on profession of faith is a little short of one hundred. Twenty-five of these have gone to their final account. Some have died in the triumphs of faith, and we humbly hope and trust that they are among the blessed, in the kingdom of our common Father. A number (as it was natural to expect from converts out of heathenish darkness) have apostatized from Christianity, and returned to their former courses. The proportion of these is not probably more than one in ten. Between sixty and seventy are now connected with some of the mission churches. A few only have removed to Allegany, Tuscarora, while the remainder still live on this reservation.

The effect of the gospel in promoting morality and civilization, may be learned in part from the fact that the public worship of God has been steadily maintained ever since the organization of the church, with members ranging from fifty to one hundred, and sometimes one hundred and fifty and two hundred as regular hearers of the word. A Sabbath school has been sustained a considerable share of the time. Many copies of the Holy Scriptures, and the New Testament, together with tracts, Sabbath school books, temperance papers, and religious periodicals, having been circulated among the children and youth. Temperance societies have been patronized by nearly all the chiefs and leading men on the reservation. Pledges have been circulated and received the signatures of a large majority of the population, of all parties, on the Washingtonian plan.

Day schools for teaching the English language have been kept in operation almost without interruption for more than twenty years, under the patronage of the A. B. C. F. M.

During the thirteen years that I have superintended these schools, nearly thirty different persons have engaged for a longer or shorter time, as teachers. For the past year there have been four schools under the patronage of the American Board, and one under the Society of Friends. The whole number who have been instructed in the five schools is probably not far from one hundred and twenty-five. The attendance of a part has been very irregular, sometimes attending no school at all. Several of the earliest pupils in the mission schools are now heads of families, well informed, industrious, frugal, temperate and religious, and in good circumstances. Some are interpreters, some teachers of schools, and others engaged in transacting the business of the nation.

You can, sir, best judge of the influence of the gospel in promoting worldly prosperity, when you have fully completed the census which is now being taken. When you count up the framed houses, and barns, the horses, cattle, sheep and hogs, the acres of improved land, with the wagons, buggies and sleighs, clocks and watches, and the various productions of agriculture, you can easily conceive the difference between the present, and thirty years ago. I suppose there was not then a framed building of any description, and scarcely a log house, properly so called, no teams, no roads, no ploughed land, and but small patches of corn, beans and squashes. What an astonishing change!

As to the capacity of Indian children for improvement, my own impression is that there is no essential difference between them and white children. The fact that Indian children usually make slow progress in studying English books, can be accounted for in three ways: 1. They generally have little or no assistance from their parents at home. 2. They are irregular in their attendance on schools, for want of order and discipline on the part of parents. 3. Being ignorant of the English language, it is a long time before they comprehend fully the instruction of their teachers.

These circumstances operate to make the school room a very dull and uninteresting place to the teacher, and the reflex influence gives the scholar the same appearance. When they can once rise above these circumstances, and overcome these obstacles, they make good proficiency in their studies.

Believing that these statements cover the ground of your inquiries, I subscribe myself, dear sir,

Respectfully and truly yours,

ASHER BLISS.

LETTER FROM REV. WILLIAM HALL TO H. R. SCHOOLCRAFT.

Allegany Mission, Sept. 8th, 1845.

DEAR SIR: — Your inquiries in relation to the state of religion, education, etc., among the Indians of this reservation, if I rightly understand them, are briefly answered as follows:

Christianity very much prospered here during the four years next preceding the past.

The number of church members during that period was

nearly tripled, and very encouraging additions were made to their knowledge and zeal. But the past year has been one of stupidity and drought.

There has, however, been four additions from the Indians made to the church, by profession of faith, and two whites.

The present number of Indian members is about one hundred and fifteen. The number of whites is eight. Seven of the Indian members are under censure.

I have sustained three schools during the past summer, in which about eighty Indian children have been more or less taught. One of these schools, whose whole number is only about thirty, gives an average attendance of nearly twenty-five. In this neighborhood the population is sufficiently compact for a farming community, and the younger parents are partially educated.

In the other neighborhoods, the population is very sparse, and the parents very ignorant. The consequence is, that the daily attendance falls short of one half the whole number of scholars, and cannot be called regular at that. Many do not get to school earlier than half past eleven, and very few earlier than ten, and half-past ten. Those who attend regularly, evince a capacity to acquire knowledge, equaling the whites, and one of our schools will suffer nothing, in comparison with common country schools.

I am, dear sir,   Yours, &c.,

WILLIAM HALL.

LETTER FROM REV. GILBERT ROCKWOOD TO HENRY R. SCHOOLCRAFT.

Tuscarora Mission, August 1, 1845.

SIR: — In the following communication you can make use of such statements as you may deem proper. If all the statements should not be necessary for your official objects, yet they may be interesting to you as an individual.

This mission was commenced about fifty years since, under the care of the " New York Missionary Society." It was transferred to the " United Foreign Mission Society," in 1821, and to the " American Board of Com. for Foreign Missions," in 1826.

The church was organized in 1805, with five persons. The whole number of native members who have united since its organization is one hundred and twenty-three. The present number of native members is fifty-three; others five, total fifty-eight.

Between July 1st, 1844, and July 1st, 1845, there were only three admissions, two by profession, and one by letter.

About one-third of the population attend meeting on the Sabbath. Their meeting house was built by themselves, with a little assistance from abroad.

They have also a school house, the expense of which was nearly all defrayed by themselves. There is but one school among them, which is kept the year through, with the exception of the vacations. The teacher is appointed by the American Board. The number of scholars the past year, is not far from 50.

I have been among these Indians now nearly eight years. I can see that there has been an advance, both in their moral and physical condition.

It is within the memory of many now living among them, when drunkenness was almost universal; now, comparatively, few are intemperate. A majority of the chiefs, are decidedly temperance men, and exert a salutary influence. They have a temperance society, and hold frequent meetings. They utterly forbid the traffic in intoxicating drinks on their own soil.

The marriage relation is being better understood by them, and more appreciated. More of the young men and women enter into the marriage relation, in the regular christian way, than a few years ago. Four couple have been regularly married the past year. Number of deaths, 8; an unusual number since I have been among them.

There is besides the church, above referred to, a Baptist church, organized a few years since, the particulars of which, I am unable to give. For any information you may wish respecting it, I would refer you to James Cusick, their minister.

On the whole, there is much to encourage the philanthropist and the christian in labors for the good and well being of the Indians here, although we meet with many obstacles and difficulties in the way.

They are becoming more and more industrious in their habits, as the appearance of their farms, and the amount of produce, and their personal appearance will testify.

With these brief statements, I subscribe myself,

Yours, truly,

GILBERT ROCKWOOD.

APPENDIX

TO

PIONEER LIFE; OR, THIRTY YEARS A HUNTER.

———

By A. MONROE AURAND, JR.

WHO WAS " PHILIP TOME? "

THERE may have been many persons who have asked this
question; we have no doubt of that. We asked the same
question ourselves, for a long time. Fact is, we didn't give
up the question until we were fortunate enough to secure
for a short time, a copy of the book entitled *Pioneer Life;
or, Thirty Years a Hunter;* being scenes and adventures
in the life of Philip Tome, etc.

The scarcity of the book made it almost impossible to get
a starting point, with which to begin any research for information as to Philip Tome, or any of his name. Eventually we were privileged to examine a copy, to find that Philip
Tome "was born in Dauphin county, near Harrisburg, in
1782."

Completing a study of it, with its detailed accounts of
hunting deer, capturing elk alive, etc., we became more or
less exercized, fearing that we might be reading "stories" of
adventures, with only a grain of truth. We then commenced
a thorough research of various bibliography, and were finally
convinced that Tome, in giving the dates, streams, names of
men and places, mileage, etc., that he did, must also have
given more than a grain of truth in his account.

Our first object was to satisfy ourselves as to whether
there was any one by the name of Tome living in Dauphin
county at the time he claims birth. There appeared none
of similar spelling in the Dauphin county records available
to us for the years at the close of the 1700's. A search
through assessment lists for Paxton township, Dauphin county, for 1785, reveals the name "Jacob Toma," being that of
the father of Philip Tome. The same name appears on said
list for the year 1786, but in 1787 it has disappeared. From
that fact it would appear that the Assessor made his rounds
early enough in 1786 to get the elder Toma on his list, for
it was in that year that Philip says they moved to Farris
creek, Northumberland county, and where they remained
for four months.

"Farris" creek does not find its way into print, therefore
we are at a loss to know just where it was. From the number
of miles given, however, it would appear that the elder Toma
had gone up the West Branch far enough to have passed
Williamsport, and from the similarity of the sound of "Far-

ris" and "Larry's" creek, we are inclined to place his residence in the vicinity of the latter stream.

Of Jacob Toma's (Tome) intention to settle in the neighborhood of Pine creek, years before he eventually did so, we have no doubt, for he had a survey made of some 400¼ acres of land along the West Branch, as shown by the following, which we copy from the official Land Records in the Department of Internal Affairs, at Harrisburg:

"A Draught of a tract of Land called ———— situate in Nittony Valley adjoining land of William Webb and others in Bald Eagle township in the county of Northumberland, survey'd on the 25th day of November 1785 for Jacob Tome by virtue of his warrant dated the seventeenth day of December 1784, containing Four Hundred Acres and one Quarter with the allowances of Six P Cent for Roads &c   Jo. J. WALLIS, D. S.
  To JOHN LUKENS Esqr
              Surveyor General"

This was "returned 22 Novemr 1794" in the name of Nicholas Diehl, Patentee, showing that Jacob Tome, for some reason or other, failed to take up the original site that he wanted, and had surveyed. The reader will note that the survey was made soon after the purchase of November 5, 1768, and which was not thrown open to settlers until 1784, after another treaty at Fort Stanwix.

Nicholas Diehl, according to the 1790 Census, was a resident of Reading Borough, with 2 males under sixteen years, and 2 females.

After the short stay of four months at "Farris" creek, the Tomes moved to Cumberland county, "five miles from Harrisburg," where they remained for "two or three years." Here the Census Enumerator in the First Census Report for the newly established Republic, found them, as appears in the report for 1790, called *Heads of Families*. The census report for the eastern part of Cumberland county shows the name Jacob Toma: 1 adult male; two white males under 16 years and two white females, including heads of families. (See Tome Miscellany for names of other brothers and sisters not mentioned during the course of the narrative).

Note that the name is sometimes spelled "Toma." Philip states that his parents were of German extraction. It is no uncommon matter for father and son to· write their names differently, and this would be no exception. The father must have written it this way, for it is not likely that the Assessor in Dauphin county, and the Census Enumerator in Cumberland county, would have written it the same way, unless that was the way it was being commonly written. Col. Henry W. Shoemaker in *Allegheny Episodes,* says: "The Pennsylvania Dutch are the most adaptable race in the world, altering the spelling of their names, their genealogies and traditions with every generation." But it matters little, as to an *a* or an *e,* for the facts of the case fit so perfectly.

In 1791, Jacob, the father, purchased land up the West Branch of the Susquehanna. They arrived at the mouth of Pine creek, "six miles from their destination." Philip Tome at first glance gives one the impression that his father reached his destination, "less six miles." Probably a mistake on his part, or the printer's, for later on (page 74), he says that in "June 1801, my father with his family removed to a more settled part of the country, twenty-two miles down Pine creek, near the West Branch of the Susquehanna, and within six miles of it." On page 26 he mentions "twenty-six miles to the mouth of Pine creek." These figures would pretty generally place the first settlement of the Tome family at the Slate Run fork of Pine creek.

A perusal of any good map of Pennsylvania, or of Lycoming county, shows along the public road, and also on the New York Central railroad, leaving Jersey Shore, a town called "Tomb," about six miles from the mouth of Pine creek, which empties into the West Branch about two miles southwest of Jersey Shore. The town evidently was laid out on the site of the Tome family settlement in those parts in the year 1801. The first post office at Tomb, was established about 1851, with Henry Tomb (a son of Jacob ?), as first postmaster.

Aside from the village of Tomb's Run, or Tomb, which is located on a forked stream whose branches are also called Tomb's Run, and which empty into Pine creek, east bank, we note another stream called "Tomb Run", just south of Slate Run, and on the west bank, and a railroad called "Tomb Run Branch." Just south of the town of Cedar Run, is "Jacob Run," perhaps named for Jacob Tome?

It is our belief that the names Toma, Tome, Tomb, Thom, Thome, etc., of which there were a number of families in central and southern Pennsylvania in the late 1700's, were pretty nearly all of the same "family."

As a further record of the father's residence along Pine creek, we present, for our readers, some excerpts from the

History of Brown Township, Lycoming County, 1892, edited by John F. Meginness, one of the most careful and depend-
able writers of historical matters, in years gone by. However
accurate most of us strive to write, sometimes we err in fact
or judgment, and we must caution the reader to read carefully what Meginness has to say with regard to early settlements of Lycoming county, as follows:

"White settlers penetrated this wild region at an early date,
attracted no doubt by the fine fishing and hunting it afforded.
Jacob Lamb is credited with being the first settler at the
mouth of Slate run. He moved his family from Milton up
the river and creek in ten canoes, and reached his point of
destination in November of that year. Benjamin Lamb,
son of Jacob and Jane Lamb, was born in the month of
March, 1795, at the mouth of Slate run, and he is believed
to have been the first male white child born that far up Pine
creek.

"Jacob Lamb was an active and enterprising man. He
erected a grist and saw mill in 1796. They were small im-
provements, no doubt, but they met the demands of the
times. His mills were the first of the kind in what is now
Brown township.

"William Blackwell settled near the county line in 1805.
He was soon followed by Andrew Gamble, John Morrison,
and Jacob Warren. Philip and John Lamb, sons of the
pioneer, erected a saw mill in Black Walnut Bottom in 1811,
which was operated by them for several years, when it passed
into the hands of Bernard Duffry.

"The Tomb family was also among those who settled early
on Pine creek. Philip Tomb (Tome) in his *Pioneer Life, or
Thirty Years a Hunter,* says that in 1791 his father purchased
land far up the creek, and hired men to build a house, etc."
Meginness goes on and says "He (Philip Tome) relates some
marvelous hunting, fishing and snake stories. Panthers came
to the houses sometimes, bear prowled about, and droves of
elk were often seen crossing the creek. He describes how his
father, with the assistance of two or three others caught an
elk alive, on a bet of £250, and took it to Stephenson's tavern
near the mouth of the creek. The feat was regarded as a
very daring one among the hunters. This was the first elk
caught. It was sixteen hands high, and had horns five and
a half feet long with eleven branches.

"Mr. Tomb's (Tome's) hunting and snake stories excel
anything related by Munchausen. In course of time he sold
out, and crossing the Alleghanies, located in Warren county,

[146]

where he died (1855). Members of the Tomb family still reside on Pine creek, but they are not given to relating such wonderful stories as their great ancestor."

Meginness either did not know or realize, while editing the *History of Brown Township,* that the names Lamb and Tomb meant the same, Tome, or else permitted one of the most remarkable coincidences of modern history to creep by without mention of it. We suspect a discrepancy in his remarks just previous, where he refers to the Lamb people, and our answer is that in ordinary long-hand writing the word *Lamb* and the word *Tomb* are so much alike that editors, and printers alike, are apt to err, and to be unable in such words as this, to read aright! Suffice it to say that there were hardly in this case, a man by the name of Jacob Lamb, and also one Jacob Tomb, who left Milton and moved up the West Branch to Pine creek; nor were there two persons who hired ten canoes, moving up Pine creek and reaching their destination (Slate Run) in November (20th) of that year (1791)! Nor two sons, named Benjamin, born in March, 1795, at Slate Run.

Meginness suddenly drops saying nice things about the Lamb family, which to all appearances seems to have been none other than the Tomb (Tome) family. He takes up the narrative with Philip Tome "whose hunting and snake stories excel anything related by Munchausen." From here on Meginness has the story of Philip Tome all right, the latter having moved to Warren county, as stated. But the West Branch historian might have been more kind to Tome, who has been recalled by Col. Parker, and others, to have been all of what Tome says of himself: "One who, in all the scenes of border life was never conquered by man or animal."

Col. Henry W. Shoemaker, in *Extinct Pennsylvania Animals,* 1917, writes: "Philip Tome, in his *Thirty Years a Hunter,* tells of Rice Hamlin killing a panther on the Tiadaghton weighing 200 pounds. About 175 pounds was a good average weight for a mature Pennsylvania Lion. Tome, who also was probably the greatest of all Pennsylvania hunters of big game, has recorded many of his hunting adventures in a book entitled *Thirty Years a Hunter.* He was a sportsman as well as hunter, never killing recklessly. Though he makes no recapitulation of panthers which fell to his unerring bullets, his descendants estimate that he killed at least 500 of these noble animals. One of his grandsons, George L. Tome, a noted hunter, resides at Corydon, in Warren county."

Again in *Allegheny Episodes,* by Col. Shoemaker, we read
that among the early settlers in Warren county, "were the
family of Philip Tome, that indomitable Indian-looking nimrod, author of *Thirty Years a Hunter,* whose prowess in the
forests of Northern Pennsylvania will never be forgotten
while memory of the big game days lasts." In the narrative
from which the previous quotation is taken, we also read:
"Philip Tome and even old Cornplanter himself tried his best
to save him," etc.

The writer of the present Appendix to Tome's book, has
"run down" nearly every name mentioned in *Pioneer Life,*
and we shall let the reader judge from our offerings whether
or not Philip Tome would have been as inaccurate with
respect to his hunting stories, etc., as he was accurate with
his names of streams, places, years, and especially of his neighbors and hunting companions.

Philip Tome must have been fairly well read, enjoyed a
good command of English, and been possessed of no little
of the "ordinary common sense," and in his introduction cau-
tions the reader, saying that "truth is often more strange
than fiction." He probably realized that a life spent almost
entirely in the forest of the undiminished game days, hunting, fishing, etc., that his experiences would far exceed those
of the average hunter and sportsman.

To have been an interpreter for Cornplanter and others,
shows that the savage, or half-civilized red man must have
had an implicit faith in the character, integrity and honesty
of Tome.

The names of many of those with whom Tome went on
hunting expeditions would seem to be recognized now to
be among those of fairly well-to-do gentlemen, business men,
and others who stood out in a prominent way in the pioneer
days. It would not have been so easy for us to show as
many of them elsewhere in this Appendix, as it has been
our pleasure to place there for the reader, if they had not
been of the aggressive, progressive and prominent type.

We have no doubt that Tome's experiences were just about
as narrated by him — that being true and unusual, they
are stranger than fiction.

In the *History of Warren County,* by Schenck and Rann,
Chapter XLIX, writing of the history of Corydon township,
we read:

"Corydon township was erected by order of the court on
the 20th of March, 1846, from territory then recently set

off from McKean county. It consists of a long narrow strip of land occupying the extreme northeastern corner of the county, and is bounded north by Cattaraugus county, N. Y., east by McKean county, south by McKean county, and west by Kinzua and the Allegheny river, separating it from Elk township. The drainage is furnished entirely by the Allegheny river and its numerous tributary streams, such as Cornplanter run, Whiskey run, Tracy run, Willow creek and Sugar creek.

"There was no settlement in the present limits of the township until as late as 1827. In 1817 James Richards passed through the land on his way to Cincinnati, and his daughter, Mrs. Lucinda Morrison, is now a resident of Corydon. The first settler in town was undoubtedly Philip Tome. * * * As early as 1816 Philip Tome was living near the present site of Kinzua, but he soon went away and did not return to this part of the State until 1827, when he came to the territory now in Corydon from Lycoming county, and built a rude shanty for a temporary dwelling place, on ground now in the center of the road which terminates between the store on the village corner and Hale's Hotel. He came down the river in a canoe, striking across from Canoe Place to the river. He died on the 30th of April, 1855. A year previous to his death he wrote and published an interesting book entitled *Pioneer Life, or Thirty Years a Hunter*, which is filled with his own adventures, some of them of the most thrilling description. He was a great hunter, and was for fifteen years interpreter for Cornplanter and Governor Blacksnake, Indian chiefs on the Allegheny river, and familiar characters to the students of the early history of Pennsylvania. Philip Tome's eldest son and second child, John C. Tome, was the first male white child born in town. The first female child born in town was Martha Forbes, daughter of Abel Morrison. The descendants of Philip Tome in Corydon and other parts of the county and State are very numerous."

"William Case, father of Squire Case, immigrated to this town very soon after the settlement of Philip Tome, and built his house about ten rods north of the hotel. He married a daughter of Philip Tome, and is now living, having survived his wife. Contemporary with Abel Morrison were his brother Rice Morrison, who settled about sixty rods below where the ferry now crosses the river, where he died only a few years ago, and Russell M. Freeman, who built his house on the east side of the street, near the present ferry, and about

on the site of Flavius Morrison's house. After a number of
years he moved away. Several years after this early settlement, Ira Butler and George Smith lived on Butler's Run
in the wood on the eastern part of the present farm of
George W. Tome, and there they undertook to make brick,
without very flattering success, however, and after the lapse
of a few unpropitious years they emigrated."

Philip Tome appears by these references to have been recognized by historians of the northern part of the State, as more
than an ordinary hunter. We quote from a statement by
Colonel Parker, of Gardeau, McKean county, Pa., a famous
hunter in his day, which followed somewhat after the years
of Tome. Colonel Parker is an authority. He says in Mc-
Knight's *History of Northwestern Pennsylvania:*
"The biggest set of elk antlers ever captured in the Pennsylvania woods was secured in the Kettle creek country by
Major Isaac Lyman, Philip Tome, George Ayres, L. D. Spoff-
ard, and William Wattles. Philip Tome was a great hunter,
and the famous interpreter for Cornplanter and Blacksnake,
the great Indian chiefs. He came over from Warren county
to help Major Lyman capture an elk alive, and the party
started in on the first snow, with plenty of ropes and things.
They camped, but the elks were in such big herds that they
couldn't get a chance at a single buck for more than a week.
Then they got the biggest one they ever saw and gave chase
to him. They started him from his bed on Yocum Hill.
The dogs took him down Little Kettle creek to Big Kettle,
and up that two or three miles. There the elk came to bay
on a rock. He kept the dogs at a distance until the hunters
came up, when he left the rock and started away again.
Tome, knowing the nature of the elk, said that all they
had to do was to wait and the elk would return to the rock.
They dropped poles and fitted up nooses. They waited nearly
half a day, and then they heard the buck coming crashing
through the woods, down the mountain-sides, the dogs in
full cry. He mounted his rock again. The hunters he did
not seem to mind, but the dogs he fought fiercely. While
he was doing that the hunters got the nooses over his immense horns and anchored him to surrounding trees. They
got the elk alive to the Allegheny river, and floated him on
a raft to Olean Point. From there they travelled with him
through New York State to Albany, exhibiting him with
much profit, and at Albany he was sold for five hundred
dollars. That elk stood sixteen hands high and had antlers

six feet long, and eleven points on each side, the usual number of points being nine on a side."

Orlo J. Hamlin, (1803-1880), who was not likely any close relative, if at all, to Rice Hamlin, kept notes on the history of early McKean county in the 1800's, and we quote from him as follows: "1800 (about), Corydon township settled by Philip Tome and others from the West Branch of the Susquehanna * * 1810-12 (about), Hamilton township settled by George Morrison and others of the West Branch of the same river * * "

TOME MISCELLANY

Mrs. Carrie B. (Tomb) Sides, of Jersey Shore, July 7, 1928, informs us that she can add but little to our account of Philip Tome, except that "there is a story of Jacob Tomb having a pair of elk broken to the harness which he drove; this was January 1st, 1800."

Mrs. Sides adds: "My father's name was John Snyder Tomb. Father had a second cousin by the name of Jacob Tome, of Port Deposit, Maryland, who built the Tome Institute. He always spelled his name "Tome." Our branch of the family used the *b*. "Tomb" I believe was the original way. I know that my grandfather, George Tomb, came from Milton; he settled on Pine Creek. Tomb's Run was named for that family. Father's Uncle Henry Tomb lived at Tomb's Run; he has a grandson living at Tomb's Run, by the name of Lewis Tomb. There was another brother who lived in Tiffin, Ohio, by the name of Benjamin Tomb; he had two sons, Thomas and George; they are all dead. My Aunt, who is Miss Amanda Tomb, lives at Bryn Athyn, Pa., with a niece, Mrs. John Beatty."

It may be of interest to our readers to know that there is a "Jacob Tome Institute," one of the finest preparatory schools in America, located at Port Deposit, Maryland. An inquiry brought the following reply from the Director of the Tome School, Dr. Murray P. Brush: "So far as we know Jacob Tome (founder of Tome School), had no connection with Philip Tome. The baptismal certificate of Jacob Tome gives him as the son of Christian and of Christiana Thom, and the date August 13, 1810. The place of his birth was Manheim township, (York county ?), Pa."

[151]

In York township, York county, 1790 Census, we note the name Christan Them, head of family, with 3 males under 16 years, and 2 females. The close similarity of this, with the name given as father of Jacob Tome, may serve to show the York county and Maryland relationship of the various families called Tome.

Mr. George Tomb Bush, of Bellefonte, Pa., informs us that "Jacob Tome, (also spelled Thom; and a southern branch spelled Toombs, and since family name spelled Tome), at one time lived in Dauphin county, about 1782, where Philip was born. Jacob Tome died in Northumberland county at the age of fifty, but cannot name the date; probably not long after 1800.

"Jacob Tomb's first wife is unknown, but had the following children, named John and Jacob. The second wife was a Jane Snyder, who had the following children, viz: Philip, George, Mary Elizabeth, Catherine, Benjamin, Henry. Mary Elizabeth married Andrew Gamble, and Catherine married James Gamble, well known names of Lycoming county. Henry married Ann Blackwell. George married Jane Humes and lived at Jersey Shore. George and Benjamin became big government contractors, building dams in the river; canals, bridges, etc. George built the famous "Camel Back" bridge at Harrisburg, as well as many miles of the first Pennsylvania canals from Harrisburg to Lock Haven, and several dams between for supplies of water for same.

"Jane Snyder, whom Jacob married (secondly), was an aunt of the afterwards Governor Simon Snyder."

Mr. J. M. English, Jersey Shore, Pa., descended from one of the earliest settlers in Lycoming county, communicates the following: "Numerous stories are told of the prowess of the early settlers in the Pine Creek Valley. These fellows were not without their love of adventure and excitement. It is told by the oldest living citizens that one man who had an idea that he was a stronger one than his neighbor went to him to try conclusions with him just for the fun of it. He found his man at his shaving horse making shingles, and stated his errand. "That suits me," said the shingle-maker. A short time later as they shook hands "good-bye," the man who had come off second-best said, "that's settled and I won't have to worry over it any longer."

"Another man who had some such suspicion in his mind

went to try conclusions with a man named Philip Tome, but after seeing Tome take up a barrel of cider and drink out of the bunghole, forgot to state his errand and went back home.

"In regard to the abundance of fish and game of that period mentioned by Philip Tome, Claudius English and a companion as late as 1825 went up the creek on a hunting trip. They hunted at Blackwell's, and in two days' time killed ten deer, two bears, and an elk. These they loaded on a "dog-raft" and brought them home.

"The first permanent settler in the Pine Creek Valley was John English, who bought an island of 29 acres and some odd square rods, and built on it in 1784. He lived there almost continuously until old age made it necessary for him to accept a home with his son William, (known by all as Uncle "Billy"), at English Centre, Pa. He died while on a visit to his daughter, Mrs. Thomas Ramsey, 2nd, at Ramseyville, Pa., and is buried on English Island, the land he bought and lived on. A memorial erected by the Antes Fort Chapter of the D. A. R. marks his grave.

"His son Claudius, the hunter mentioned above, was born in 1785, and was the first white child born in the valley."

In the *History of Lycoming County*, 1892, we note the following:

"Opposite the mouth of Cedar Run John S. Tomb and Son operate a steam saw mill on a large scale."

"There are some good farms along Pine Creek. * * * The Tomb family—one of the oldest—is well represented by numerous descendants of the venerable patriarch, Henry Tomb, who did so much to develop the township (Watson).

In Brown Township, we read: "Churches and Schools:— The first religious exercises were held at the house of Jacob Lamb (Tomb), in 1805, by Rev. William Hay.

"The first school was opened and taught by John Campbell, a Scotchman, at Black Walnut Bottom in 1806, and tradition says that he taught seven days in the week."

NEWSPAPER CLIPPINGS.

Mr. and Mrs. I. C. Tomb, of Corning, N. Y., Mrs. J. M. Gohl, and Miss Emma Tomb, of Washington avenue, attended the funeral of Mr. W. B. Tomb, at Slate Run, on Sunday. — Jersey Shore *Herald*, July 2, 1928.

TOMES IN WARREN COUNTY, PA., 1850 CENSUS

The following names may, with almost a certainty, be counted as relatives, if not descendants, of Philip Tome, in Corydon township, Warren county, Pa., in 1850:

Age	Name	Occupation	Born
68	Philip Tome,	farmer	Pa.
64	Mary Tome		Pa.
22	John Tome	farmer	Pa.
26	Hiram Tome,	lumberman	Pa.
22	Annette Tome		N.Y.
10	Adelbert Tome		Pa.
41	Benjamin Tome,	lumberman	Pa.
34	Cynthia Tome		N.J.
15	Henry Tome,	lumberman	Pa.
14	Esther Tome		Pa.
11	Juliet Tome		Pa.
10	Sarah Tome		Pa.
6	Nancy I. Tome		Pa.
4	George Tome		Pa.
2	O. F. Tome		Pa.
32	George Tome,	lumberman	N.Y.
29	Ann Tome		Conn.
6	Rebecca Tome		Pa.

In 1878, in the *Historical Atlas of Warren County*, we find in the Corydon township directory, the following names, presumably all descendants of Philip Tome: Hiram Tome, lumberman; George L. Tome, farmer, with 29 acres; and G. W. Tome, farmer, with 30 acres, all with address at Corydon. Fifty years later (1928), this list of Tomes ought to be greatly augmented.

WARREN COUNTY RECORDS

Deed.—Vol. D: 475.

Enoch Gilman and wife (Permilla) to Philip Tome. Consideration $20.00. One sixth of island "being the first Island below the York State line containing two acres and seventeen perches." Also one fourth of water privileges "over and above the water privileges granted by the said party of the first part to Russell M. Freeman & Abel Morrison for a single mill."

Witnesses—Wm. Gibbs and Josiah Hall. Date—August 9, 1830; Acknowledged—August 9, 1830; Recorded—March 24, 1832.

Deed.—Vol. D: 564.

Philip Tome of Corydon, McKean county, Pa., to Aaron Wheeler of Bustall, Ontario county, N. Y. Consideration $1500.00. Sawmill on island in Allegheny river in Warren county. About a mile below the New York State line. Fourth mill from east shore and *west?* mill in the establishment built by Keyes and Convers. With water privileges. Also undivided one sixth of island to which dam of mill is attached with one fourth of all water privileges over and above those granted by Enoch Gilman to Russell M. Freeman and Abel Morrison.

Witnesses—Wm. Gibbs and James L. Baker. Date—March 26, 1832; Acknowledged—April 5, 1832; Recorded—September 27, 1832.

Deed.—Vol. E: 204.

Philip Tome of Catteraugus County, N. Y., to Jonathan Thompson, of McKean county, Pa. Consideration $1200.00. One half of shore mill on McKean shore and one eighth of island in the Allegheny river on which the mill dam is attached opposite the village of Corydon "it being the same property contracted for, between the parties verbally, some time in June one thousand eight hundred and thirty, and followed immediately by possession on the part of Thompson and not being able to make a good title until now."

Witnesses—Wm. Gibbs and Morris L. Gibbs. Date—Feb. 19, 1833; Acknowledged—Feb. 19, 1833; Recorded—Sept. 5, 1833.

SHORT SKETCH OF CORNPLANTER

This history would be incomplete, without some additional notice of the earliest settler of Warren county, Gy-ant-wa-chia, alias John O'Bail, alias the "Cornplanter." He was a distinguished chief of the Seneca tribe of Indians, one of the confederate Six Nations, celebrated before and during the Revolutionary War. Cornplanter was a half-breed, the contemporary of Washington, about the same age, a valiant warrior of his tribe, and of superior sagacity and eloquence.

He fought on the side of the French, during the French and English struggle for the northwest of this continent, commencing with the battle of the Monongahela, on the 9th of July, 1755, and resulting in Braddock's defeat and death. During the Revolutionary War, he, as a chief of one of the Six Nations, was in league with, and fought on the side of the British. Immediately on the close of the war, being deserted by his British allies, he saw that the true policy for his tribe and race was to accept the situation, and make friends with their future masters. This he hastened to do, and was efficient in bringing the Six Nations into friendly treaties with the government. He was himself one of the negotiators and signers to the treaties of Fort Stanwix and Fort Harmar, ceding large districts of land to the United States.

He maintained his allegiance most faithfully and efficiently during the Indian war, from 1790 to 1794, rendering valuable assistance to the general government, and in the protection of the western frontiers of Pennsylvania. For these services, among other rewards, he received from Pennsylvania permission to select one thousand five hundred acres of land from her unappropriated territory, for himself and his posterity.

Among his selections he chose for his own occupancy a tract of six hundred and forty acres of land on the west bank of the Alleghany river, fourteen miles above Warren, together with two large adjacent islands. Here he located himself and family about 1791, and resided until his death in 1836, at the age of one hundred or upwards, and here his family and descendants to the number of eighty-five still reside. In 1866 the Legislature of Pennsylvania authorized the erection of a monument to the memory of the old chieftain, which was done under the supervision of the writer, at a cost of $550, and now marks the grave of one of the bravest, noblest and truest specimens of the aboriginal race. Three of his children were present at the dedication of his monument in 1866 — the last of whom died in 1874, at the age of about one hundred years. — Hon. S. P. Johnson, in the *Historical Atlas of Warren County,* 1878.

CORNPLANTER INDIANS AND THEIR SCHOOLS

The Cornplanter Indians are a family of the Seneca tribe, occupying a reservation of between eight and nine hundred acres on the west bank of the Alleghany river, in the northeastern portion of Warren county. They are the descendants of John O'Bail, a half-breed, better known as the celebrated Cornplanter. Cornplanter was the head chief of his nation, and appears to have been the most powerful and influential chief of the Six Nations. Cornplanter gave his eldest son a good education, which he used for the basest purpose of fraud, involving often the interests of his father, who appears to have attributed all to his son's education. This circumstance gave rise to a strong prejudice in Cornplanter's family against education, which, for a time, thwarted all efforts to establish and maintain schools among them.

In the year 1820 Samuel Oldham, a Quaker (probably a Presbyterian, rather than Quaker, on account of Cornplanter's dislike for the Quakers whose teachings did not agree with Cornplanter's ideas—See page 36—A.M.A.) minister, established a private school in a log house, and taught more or less for nearly fifteen years. No more school was had among the Indians until 1856, when Rev. L. L. Spencer, then County Superintendent, was riding along the east side of the river, and seeing several Indian children, conceived the idea of starting a school for them. He drew up a petition and presented it to the State Legislature through Hon. D. Lott, then a member for the county, who secured the passage of an Act to establish a school among the Cornplanter Indians, and $100 was annually appropriated for its maintenance until 1872 or 1873, when the appropriation was increased to $300 per year.

In 1857 the chief procured $200 from his nation for the purpose of building a school-house, and that year a good frame school-house was built. Miss Julia L. Tomes was the first teacher. Messrs. Benjamin Tomes, J. E. Woodbeck, and Rice Morrison rendered essential aid to Rev. L. L. Spencer in the establishment of this school. The Indians at present take pride in their school, and it is in a flourishing condition. Mr. Marsh Pierce, an Indian, is the chief educational man among them at the present time. — N. R. Thompson, Esq., in the *Historical Atlas of Warren County*, 1878.

LYCOMING COUNTY

Lycoming county was taken from Northumberland by the act of 13th April, 1795. It then comprised all the north-western part of the State beyond Mifflin, Huntingdon, and Westmoreland counties, and as far as the Alleghany river. Its limits have been curtailed by the successive establishment of Centre, Armstrong, Indiana, Clearfield, Jefferson, Mc-Kean, Potter, Tioga and Clinton counties.

The population of the county was originally composed of Scotch-Irish and Quakers, from the lower counties of the State, and their descendants still occupy the valleys, together with many Germans and others from Pennsylvania and New York.

The purchase of land by the proprietary government at the treaty of Fort Stanwix (present site of Rome, N. Y.), Nov. 5, 1768, then known as the "new purchase," opened the way for the settlement of the whites on the West Branch. Previous to this date, the valley had been occupied by a few straggling bands of Shawanee and Monsey Indians, who had retired from the lower valley of the Susquehanna; and occasionally parties of the Senecas came down to hunt, or more commonly to fall upon the defenceless families of the frontier. The Indians dwelling here were visited by David Brainerd, and by the Moravian missionaries, about the years 1744 to 1746.

During several years previous to the purchase, the Scotch-Irish rangers of the Kittatinny valley had often visited the valley of the West Branch, extending their excursions as far up as the Big Island, for the purpose of cutting off hostile parties of Indians, and their practised eyes had not failed to notice the extreme fertility and beauty of the land. Accordingly, no sooner was the purchase known, than a crowd of these adventurers flocked in, and when the land-office was opened in April following, it was besieged by a great number of applicants, and it became necessary to decide the priority of location by lottery. The purchases were limited to 300 acres for each individual, at £5 per 100 acres, and one penny per acre quit-rent. An allotment was made of 104,000 acres to the officers of the provincial regiments, who had served during the Indian campaigns, and who were desirous of settling together. Soon after the purchase of 1768, a question arose between the settlers and the government, whether Lycoming creek or Pine creek was the English name for the stream call *Tiadaghton* in the treaty; and the question remained unsettled for sixteen years, when, at another treaty at Fort Stanwix, 1784, it was learned from the Indians that Tiadaghton meant Pine creek.

Stockade forts were erected at each important settlement along the West Branch, as places of refuge for families in times of invasion. Some of these were garrisoned by continental or provincial troops; others were defended by the settlers of the neighborhood. There was a block-house near the site of Lock Haven, commanded in 1778 by Col. Long. Samuel Horn's fort was on the right bank of the West Branch a little below Chatham's mill, and 3 miles above the mouth of Pine creek. Antis' fort was also on the right bank, at the head of the Nippenose bottom.

Just above Pine creek, and north of the road to Lock Haven, is one of those ancient circular fortifications of earth, so well known in this State and Ohio. The banks are becoming gradually obliterated by the action of the elements. Near the fort, and on both sides of the creek, are ancient Indian burying-grounds, from which bones and trinkets have been occasionally disinterred by the whites. Tradition says that two hostile tribes once lived on each side of the creek.

A very flourishing settlement has recently grown up at the forks of Pine creek, eight miles northwest of Jersey Shore [Tomb's Run?]. A large double saw-mill has been erected, several stores, tavern, etc.
— Day's *Historical Collections of Penna.*

POTTER COUNTY

Potter county was separated from Lycoming, by the act of 26th March, 1804. The county comprises the high, rolling, and table-land, adjacent to the northern boundary of the State, lying on the outskirts of the great bituminous coal formation. Its streams are the sources of the Alleghany, the Genesee, and the West Branch of the Susquehanna; and a resident of the county says that all these streams head so near together, that a man in three hours may drink from waters that flow into the Gulf of St. Lawrence, the Gulf of Mexico, and the Chesapeake bay, respectively. The names of these sources are the Alleghany, the Genesee, the East branch of Sinnemahoning, Kettle creek, Pine creek, and Cowanesque creek.

The history of the early pioneers is one of extreme toil and hardship, yet health and competence have been their reward; and where they found nought but a howling wilderness, traversed only by the Indian, the bear, the wolf, the panther, the elk, and the deer, they now see cultivated fields, abounding with cattle and sheep, and an industrious population, furnished with mills, schools and manufactories. The following extracts are from the correspondence of respectable citizens of the county. An early settler, Benjamin Birt, Esq., says:

"In the year 1808 an east and west road was opened thru Potter county. Messrs. John Keating & Co., of Philadelphia, owning large tracts of land in the northwest part of the county, agreed with Isaac Lyman, Esq., to undertake the opening of the road. In the fall of 1809 Mr. Lyman came in, with several hands, and erected a rude cabin, into which he moved in March, 1810. He then had but one neighbor in the county, who was four miles distant. I moved in on the 4th May, 1811, and had to follow the fashion of the country for building and other domestic concerns,—which was rather tough, there being not a bushel of grain or potatoes, nor a pound of meat, except wild, to be had in the county; but there were leeks and nettles in abundance, which, with venison and bear's meat, seasoned with hard work and a keen appetite, made a most delicious dish. The friendly Indians of different tribes frequently visited us on their hunting excursions. Among other vexations were the gnats, a very minute but poisonous insect, that annoyed us far more than musquitoes, or even than hunger and cold; and in summer we could not work without raising a smoke around us.

"Our roads were so bad that we had to fetch our provisions 50 to 70 miles on pack-horses. In this way we lived until we could raise our own grain and meat. By the time we had grain to grind, Mr. Lyman had built a grist mill; but the roads still being bad, and the mill at some distance from me, I fixed an Indian samp-mortar to pound my corn, and afterwards I contrived a small hand-mill, by which I have ground many a bushel,—but it was hard work. When we went out after provisions with a team, we were compelled to camp out in the woods; and, if in the winter, to chop down a maple-tree for our cattle to browse on all night,— and on this kind of *long fodder* we had to keep our cattle a good part of the winter.

"When I came here I had a horse that I called *"Main dependence,"* on account of his being a good steady old fellow. He used to carry my whole amily on his back whenever we went to a wedding, a raising, a logging-bee, or to visit our neighbors, for several years,—until the increasing load comprised myself, my wife, and three children—five in all.

"We had often to pack our provisions 80 miles from Jersey Shore. Sixty miles of the road was without a house; and in the winter, when deep snows came on and caught us on the road without fire, we should have perished if several of us had not been in company to assist each other.

"The want of leather, after our first shoes were worn out, was severely felt. Neither tanner nor shoemaker lived in the county. But "necessity is the mother of invention." I made me a trough out of a big pine-tree, into which I put the hides of any cattle that died among us. I used ashes for tanning them instead of lime, and bear's grease for oil. The thickest served for sole leather, and the thinner ones, dressed with a drawing-knife, for upper leather; and thus I made shoes for myself and neighbors.

"I had 14 miles to go in winter to mill with an ox team. The weather was cold, and the snow deep; no roads were broken, and no bridges built across the streams. I had to wade the streams, and carry the bags on my back. The ice was frozen to my coat as heavy as a bushel of corn. I worked hard all day and got only seven miles the first night, when I chained my team to a tree, and walked three miles to house myself. At the second night I reached the mill. My courage often failed, and I had almost resolved to return; but when I thought of my children crying for bread, I took new courage."

Mr. John Peat, another old pioneer, in a communication in the *Forester* in 1834, says:

"It will be 23 years the 23d day of May, 1834, since I moved into Potter county. Old Mr. Ayres was in the county at that time, and had been in the county about five years alone. In the fall before I came, three families—(Benjamin Birt, Major Lyman, and a Mr. Sherman)—moved into the county. The East and West State Road was cut out the year before I moved in.

"It was very lonesome for several years. People would move in, and stay a short time, and move away again. It has been but a few years since settlers began to stick. I made some little clearing, and planted some garden seeds, etc., the first spring. We brought a small stock of provisions with us. On the 3d day of July I started, with my two yoke of oxen, to go to Jersey Shore, to mill, to procure flour. I crossed Pine creek eighty times going to, and eighty times

coming from mill, was gone eighteen days, broke two axle-
trees to my wagon, upset twice, and one wheel came off in
crossing the creek.

"Jersey Shore was the nearest place to procure provisions,
and the road was dreadful. The few seeds that I was able
to plant the first year, yielded but little produce. We however raised some half-grown potatoes, some turnips, and soft
corn, with which we made out to live, without suffering,
till the next spring, at planting time, when I planted all the
seeds that I had left; and when I finished planting, we had
nothing to eat but leeks, cow-cabbage, and milk. We lived
on leeks and cow-cabbage as long as they kept green—about
six weeks. My family consisted of my wife and two children; and I was obliged to work, though faint for want of
food.

"The first winter, the snow fell very deep. The first
winter month, it snowed 25 days out of 30; and during the
three winter months it snowed 70 days. I sold one yoke
of my oxen in the fall, the other yoke I wintered on browse;
but in the spring one ox died, and the other I sold to procure
food for my family, and was now destitute of a team, and
had nothing but my own hands to depend upon to clear my
lands and raise provisions. We wore out all our shoes the
first year. We had no way to get more,—no money, nothing
to sell, and but little to eat,—and were in dreadful distress
for want of the necessaries of life. I was obliged to work
and travel in the woods barefooted. After a while, our
clothes were worn out. Our family increased, and the children were nearly naked. I had a broken slate that I brought
from Jersey Shore. I sold that to Harry Lyman, and bought
two fawn-skins, of which my wife made a petticoat for
Mary; and Mary wore the petticoat until she outgrew it;
then Rhoda took it, till she outgrew it; then Susan had it,
till she outgrew it; then it fell to Abigail, and she wore it
out."

— Day's *Historical Collections of Penna.*

TIOGA COUNTY

Tioga county was separated from Lycoming by the Act of
25th March, 1804; in 1806 the seat of justice was established
at Wellsboro.

Until the year 1796-97, Tioga and the neighboring counties were a howling wilderness, entirely cut off from the West
Branch settlements by the lofty barrier of the Alleghany

mountains — and trodden only by the beasts of the forest, and the savage on his hostile expedition to the lower settlements. About that time a Mr. Williamson of New York, an agent for Sir William Pulteney, first opened a rough wagon road through this wilderness, across the mountains from the mouth of Lycoming creek, to the sources of the Tioga, and thence down that river to Painted Post in New York. This road was made at the expense of Sir William Pulteney for the purpose of rendering his lands in the State of New York accessible to German or other emigrants coming up from Philadelphia and Baltimore. Old Mr. Covenhoven (Crownover) of Lycoming county, and Mr. Patterson, superintended the workmen on the road, who were principally German redemptioners. This road became a great thoroughfare, and was extensively known as the "Blockhouse road," from a log-house, (called blockhauss by the Germans,) erected by Williamson near the mountains for the accommodation of travellers.

After the opening of this road, many of the pioneers from the Wyoming country, and from New England, came into the eastern part of the county, and took up lands under the Connecticut title. For quite a number of years, the uncertainty of this title gave rise to much wrangling and litigation. A Mr. Gobin, an assistant-surveyor under the Pennsylvania title, was shot in his camp, but not killed. At length the litigation was ended by the compromise at Trenton: the settlers quietly acknowledged the validity of the Pennsylvania title, and compromised their claims with the agents of the landholders from Philadelphia. A large portion of the lands, in the eastern section of the county, belonged to the Bingham estate.

Soon after the cutting of the Block-house road, Mr. John Norris, from Philadelphia, first came, about the beginning of the year 1799, to the southwestern part of the county, as an agent for Mr. Benjamin Morris, who owned lands in that region. He was accompanied by his brother-in-law, Mr. Mordecai Jackson, then a young lad. On Mr. Norris's arrival, he erected a grist and saw mill, on the waters of Little Pine creek, just within the boundary of Lycoming county. This establishment was generally known as Morris's mills. After remaining at Morris's mills for five or six years, and inducing some half dozen settlers to immigrate, Mr. Norris removed to the vicinity of the Big Marsh; and subsequently, in 1807, to within a mile of Wellsboro. The mill at that place had been built the year previous, (1806,) by Samuel

W. Fisher, of Philadelphia; and the same year the county seat
was fixed at Wellsboro. Among the first settlers, at or near
Wellsboro, besides Mr. Norris, were Benjamin W. Morris,
David Linsey, Alpheus Cheney, and Daniel Kelsey, Esq.
— Day's *Historical Collections of Penna.*

WARREN COUNTY

Warren county was taken from Lycoming county by the
act of 12th March, 1800. On the 16th March, 1819, the
county was fully organized, and the seat of justice fixed at
Warren.

Previous to the year 1827, that part of the county southeast of the Alleghany river was but little known or explored,
and the land abandoned by its owners was principally sold
for taxes; but since the titles could be perfected, settlers
have moved in, and found the region to be well timbered,
supplied with abundant water-power, and containing much
good arable land.

At Irwinville, James Harriot built the first mills, about
the year 1812, or 1813. Messrs. Faulkner, Wilson, Smith,
and Hall were the first settlers near Pine Grove, about the
years 1816-20. The McKinney family were also early settlers: John settled on Brokenstraw, and Barney and Michael
on the Conewango. Major Robert Andrews, and Messrs.
Hicks, Wilson, Youngs, and Kinnear, were also early settlers
on Brokenstraw. Most of them were lumbermen. Tomes,
an Irishman, and Daniel McQuay, also settled on Brokenstraw.

The settlement of Warren county, more than of any of the
neighboring counties, was greatly retarded by the miscon-
structions and litigation resulting from the land law of 1792,
and the peculiar management of the Holland Land Company.
— Day's *Historical Collections of Penna.*

GAZETTEER OF TOWNS, &c.

Big Marsh. Marsh creek forms the Third fork of Pine creek. The village of the same name is three miles from the fork, but Big Marsh would likely be in the vicinity of Mansfield.

Big Meadows. According to our calculations this would be in the vicinity southwest of Ansonia, in Shippen township, Tioga county.

Cold Spring. Along the Alleghany river, in New York State, about seven miles north of the State line, and about ten or twelve miles from Tome's later home, at Corydon.

Cornplanter's Town. In Corydon township, Warren Co.

Coudersport. Established in 1807. Named for a young officer of General Lafayette's staff, Major Coudert.

Dunn's Eddy. Now a town by same name. May have been named for Henry Dunn, an early settler in Warren county. There was also a Jeremiah Dunn, noted as a juryman in the famous "Hook Murder Trial," in 1824.

Four Corners. Not unlikely in the vicinity of Kane.

Franklin. Laid out under an act of 1795, in about 700 lots. Formerly Venango.

Kittanning. Built on the site of an old Indian village which was burned on the morning of the 8th of August, 1757, by Colonel, afterwards General John Armstrong.

Kittanning Block House. Concerning this, we quote from a letter from Mr. J. E. Henretta, of Kane, Pa., 1928: "I have gone over this book rather carefully and find that on one of his (Tome's) hunting expeditions he describes a night's camp on a stream approximately 17 miles from Kinzua, at a point where a small stream enters the Kinzua. Subsequent matter regarding this hunting trip clearly identifies this place as that point where Hubert Run enters the Kinzua. A little later on in a story of this same hunting trip he refers to a Block House, and Fort, built at the Cross Roads. This is undoubtedly the intersection of the military road that formerly ran through Kane, with the old Kittanning Road. In fact, he mentions the Kittanning Road in his description. The location of the Fort or Block House I have under investigation with residents of Kane at the present time and we have it pretty definitely placed as being near the water tower in this town."

Warren. By an act of 18th April, 1795, the town of Warren was directed to be laid out, to contain 300 acres.

GAZETTEER OF RIVERS, STREAMS, &c.

Cedar run. A stream which empties into Pine creek at the village of Cedar Run, northwestern Lycoming county.

Clarion river, or Great Toby's creek. Rises in Sergeant township, McKean county, and flows a southwesterly course through Jefferson county, etc., into the Alleghany at Foxburg; length, 70 miles. In 1832 it was said to be navigable for 55 miles, with boats.

Conewango creek. Rises in Chautauqua county, New York, flows southerly into Warren county, and emptying into the Alleghany at Warren; length, in Pennsylvania, 13.5 miles.

Farris creek. From its not appearing in print anywhere, would likely be none other than a mis-nomer for Larry's creek, Lycoming county.

First Fork, Pine creek. "Twelve miles," would be at the present town of Waterville; Second fork, at the town of Lloyd, Tioga county; Third fork, southwest of Ansonia, Tioga county.

Kettle creek. Rises in Elk township, southwestern Tioga county, flows circuitously through Potter and Clinton counties into West Branch Susquehanna at Westport.

Kinzua (Kenzua, Kinjua,) creek. Rises in Keating township, central McKean county, flows southwest to near Mt. Jewett, thence northwest into Warren county, to Alleghany river, emptying at Kinzua; length, 34 miles. The same; South branch, rises in Hamlin township, southwest McKean county, flowing westerly and northwesterly to Kinzua creek, near Root run; length, 12 miles.

Loyal Sock creek. Rises in Forkston township, southwestern Wyoming county, flowing westerly into Sullivan county, to Forksville, thence southwesterly into Lycoming county, to the West Branch of the Susquehanna at Montoursville; length, 59.5 miles.

Lycoming creek. Rises in Canton township, southwestern Bradford county, flowing southwesterly into Lycoming county, to West Branch Susquehanna at Williamsport; length, 34.5 miles.

Marsh creek. Rises in Duncan township, south central Tioga county, flowing northwest and southwest into Pine creek, one mile southwest of Ansonia; length, 20 miles.

Marvin's creek. Empties into Potato creek, at Smethport.

Pine creek (Tiadaghton). Formed by the junction of Cushing creek and Genesee fork, at West Pike, Pike township, eastern central Potter county; elevation 1,450 feet. The course is easterly into Tioga county to junction of Marsh creek; thence southerly into Lycoming county; thence southwesterly and southeasterly to West Branch Susquehanna river, being Clinton-Lycoming boundary for last 4.5 miles. The mouth is about 2 miles southwest of Jersey Shore. It is 72 miles in length. The drainage area is 973 square miles, embracing portions of Potter, Tioga, Lycoming and Clinton counties. The channel is sinuous, through deep, steep-sided valleys, with rough, rocky bed.

Potato creek. Formed by junction of East and West branches, in Norwich township, southeast McKean county, flowing northerly to Alleghany river, with its mouth about 1 mile south of Larabee; length, 19 miles.

Round Island. Tome, in August, 1795, with his father, and Jerry Morrison, went up Pine creek, to "Round Island." A glance at "Tanner's Map of Penna." for 1846, shows Round Islands about 1.5 miles below what is now Tiadaghton, Delmar township, Tioga county. Also—there is a "Round Island" in Clinton county, just east of the Cameron county line, on the Sinnemahoning.

Sinnemahoning creek. Formed by junction of Driftwood branch and Bennett branch, at Driftwood, flowing into Susquehanna at Keating; length 16 miles. The First fork, formed by junction of Prouty branch and Ayer Hill branch, central Potter county, flowing into Sinnemahoning creek at Sinnemahoning; length 31 miles. The First fork, East fork, has its source in Summit township, Potter county, flowing southeast to First fork, and emptying at Wharton; length, 16.5 miles.

Stony fork. A village of this name lies about 5 miles southwest of Wellsboro, on Stony fork creek, one of the branches of Babb creek, flowing into Pine creek at Lloyd.

Tioga river. Rises in Armenia township, in western Bradford county, flows southwest into Tioga county, thence northerly into New York to Chemung river. Its length in Pennsylvania is 45 miles.

Tionesta creek. Rises in Watson township, southern Warren county, flowing northeast, then southeast and southwesterly to Alleghany river, at Tionesta; length 58 miles. The same—South branch, rises in Highland township, northwest Elk county, flowing northwest through Forest county, into Warren county, to Tionesta creek, near Barnes; length, 15 miles.

Tuneungwant creek. The East and West branches rise in Lafayette township, McKean county, emptying into the main stream at Bradford; length 14.5 and 9 miles, and the main branch in Pennsylvania, 3 miles, respectively. The main branch empties into the Alleghany river in New York State, 6 miles above the line. Commonly known as "Tuna" creek.

Warry (Warrior ?) Run. In Northumberland county, but more than "two miles from the junction of the North and West Branches." Tome likely meant the stream that empties into the West Branch at Watsontown.

Young Woman's creek. Rises in Stewardson township, Potter county, flows southerly to Clinton county, emptying into the West Branch Susquehanna at North Bend; length, 16.5 miles.

BIOGRAPHICAL INDEX

AVERY, ———. Unable to find.

AYERS, GEORGE. Mr. John Peat, an old pioneer, in a communication to the *Forester*, in 1834, says: "It will be 23 years the 23d day of May, 1834, since I moved into Potter county. Old Mr. Ayres was in the county at that time, and had been in the county about five years alone. In the fall before I came, three families—(Benjamin Birt, Major Lyman and a Mr. Sherman)—moved into the county."

BURT, ———. Undoubtedly Benjamin Birt, who settled in Potter county in 1811. (See Mr. Birt's statement in the Chapter on Potter County, on page 160).

CAMPBELL, JOHN. In Conewango township, Warren county, in 1808, a John Campbell, a single man, was assessed.

CARNS, ———. The only place we could locate the name Carns, was in the 1790 Census. In Franklin township, Westmoreland county, 1790, we find listed one James Carns, with 1 male under 16 years and 1 female; two other Carns, James and John, are enumerated in Washington county, in 1790. In the *History of Venango County*, we note that in Richard township, among the early settlers (about 1800) were several members of the Karns families; later on we note the names of Abraham, Williams, Jacob, Isaac and James Karns.

DARLING, JOSEPH. In 1816 we note James Darling, in Brokenstraw township, Warren county, assessed with a saw-mill. Wm. T. Darling, of Corry, and George Darling, of Spring Creek, in 1878, were likely descendants.

GAMBLE, JAMES. Philip Tome's sister Catherine married a James Gamble (see Tome Miscellany); another sister, Mary Elizabeth, married an Andrew Gamble. We find Andrew

Gambles, heads of families, 1790 Census, in northern Mifflin county and Chester county; and a James Gamble, also a family head, in York county. Lacking more definite data it would be hazarding a guess as to which Gamble, if any of those just mentioned, moved to Lycoming county in 1805, as noted in the *History of Lycoming County.*

GEEBUCK, JOHN. Probably one of Cornplanter's trustworthy and reliable hunters, such as Tome could easily get along with.

GIBSON, WILLIAM. The nearest we can come to this name is Widow Gilson, assessed in Conewango township, Warren county, in 1816.

GOODWIN, ——. In 1806 we note a Joseph Goodwin, a single man, assessed in Warren county, with 1 cow; again in 1816. In 1808, there was assessed in Conewango township, one Jacob Goodwin, with 600 acres, 2 horses, 2 cows, 2 oxen, 2 in-lots in Warren, and ½ saw-mill.

HALFTOWN, MORRIS. One of Cornplanter's chiefs was known as Half-Town, and these two, with other chiefs, were at Philadelphia, October 29, 1790, where the former addressed the Supreme Executive Council.

HAMLIN, RICE. A man by this name taught school in Kinzua township, Warren county, after 1825. May be the same. Ten miles south of Smethport, on Potato creek, one of the branches of the Alleghany river, is the town of Hamlin.

HEWLING, THOMAS. No such name or similar name in Pennsylvania Census for 1790. Must have been a newcomer.

HOOK, JOSEPH. Search of various histories fails to reveal any Joseph Hook, but Jacob Hook has prominence on account of his trial for murder; also on account of his circulation of a large amount of doubtful paper currency on some eastern bank which had failed. Jacob Hook came to Warren county about 1812 (said Judge Wetmore), and died about 1829 or 1830.

KNAPP, JOSHUA. We note a town in New York State, just across the line, called Knapp's Creek. In 1797 Moses Knapp, Samuel Scott, Joseph and Andrew Barnett, removed from their home at the mouth of Pine creek, to near the present site of Brookville, at Mill creek, sometimes called Port Barnett. Here they erected, after some "labor" troubles with the Indians, a saw mill. The boards were run to what is now Pittsburgh, in 1801. Moses Knapp was the pioneer pilot. "Joshua" and "Moses" Knapp must have been relatives from the uniform use of Bible names. We suspect that Moses might have been the older of the two living in 1800, from the fact that at that time Joshua had "never shot an elk," while Moses was then in "big business." Moses Knapp moved to what is now called Baxter, in the spring of 1821, and while cutting timber he got a foot and leg crushed so that his limb had to be amputated above the knee, the operation being performed by Drs. Stewart of Indiana, and Rankin, of Clarion county, that same year. We note a village called Knapp about four miles south of Wellsboro.

LYMAN, MAJOR ISAAC. "Major Isaac Lyman, the agent of the Keating (Land) Company, came in 1809 and founded Lymansville, where he built the first grist-mill constructed from lumber cut with a whip-saw on the Keating farm."— Hon. M. E. Olmstead, in *Lycoming County Centennial Proceedings*.

MADDOCK, ——. A "Richard Madocks" lived in Northumberland county, 1790, with 1 adult, one male under 16, and four females; also a "Peter Maddocks," in the same county, with 1 adult male and two females.

McKEAN, ROBERT. The only names of Robert McKean we find are in the 1790 Census: 1 adult male, 1 male under 16 years, and 2 females, in Washington county; and 2 adult males, 2 males under 16 years and 1 female, in Mifflin county.

McMULLEN, JAMES. We find names such as this in Cumberland, Bucks, Chester, Washington and York counties in 1790, but none in Northumberland, nor near the present limits of Lycoming county at the time mentioned, 1796.

MILLS, JOHN. Listed in the census for 1790, with 2 adult males, 2 males under 16 years, and 4 females, in Northumberland county. On page 669, *History of Lycoming County*, we read: "It is claimed that the first white child born at the mouth of the run (Tomb's) was Abigail Mills, daughter of James Mills, in 1786."

MORRISON, JERRY. On page 665, *History of Lycoming County*, we read: "Among other early settlers may be mentioned Jeremiah Morrison" (likely about 1790-95). Jerry Morrison is listed in Heads of Families, 1790 Census, in Northumberland county, with 6 adult males, one male under 16 years and one female.

About the year 1795 the venerable James Morrison (who died in the year 1840, at the age of 104), took up the large island at the mouth of the Kinjua creek; he was also owner of Morrison's Island, at the mouth of Morrison's creek, a few miles above Warren. A town, Morrison, in western Mc-

Kean county, is probably named for him. He is also listed in the 1790 Census, with 2 adult males, 4 males under 16 years, and 2 females, next to the entry of "Jerry Morrison," which see. Also, in same county, and same page of census report, we find Ephraim Morrison, with 1 adult male, 1 male under 16 years, and 4 females, and Samuel Morrison, Senr., with 2 adult males, 1 male under 16 years, and 2 females. Thus we find any number of Morrisons around in 1790.

MORRISON, GEORGE. This being in 1821, and so many, many Morrison families about, we did not attempt to check this name, though it may belong to the family of James Morrison, of Warren county.

SEAMAN, WALTER. This name appears among the list of traverse jurors for the first Court of Quarter Sessions in Warren county, on Monday, November 29, 1819. His name appears on several other occasions as that of juror in important trials in that county.

SILVERHEELS, GEORGE. He is said to have been one of the Indian prophets, and also to be a brother of Chief Cornplanter.

SMITH, ALEXANDER. Is listed in Heads of Families, 1790 Census, with 1 adult, 1 male under 16 years and 2 females, in Northumberland county.

TANNER, ——. Tome evidently meant Archibald Tanner, who was one of the first merchants in Warren. Tanner brought his store goods from the Ohio Valley, up the Alleghany in a keel boat. Tanner built, in 1816, the little one-story frame building which stood on the banks of the river, at Warren, for so many years. Mr. Tanner was the first treasurer of Warren county.

THOMPSON, ROBERT. Was assessed in Brokenstraw township, Warren county, in 1816. There is a town by the name of Thompson's Station, in Warren county, probably also known as Gray's Eddy, in old river transportation days.

WHITCOMB, MARSHALL. Not found in any bibliography. However, in Warren county, in 1878, there were living Messrs. Joel, C. K., N. J., E., and G. Whitcomb, who undoubtedly were descendants of Marshall Whitcomb.

WHITMORE, ——. In 1816, there appears on the assessment list for Brokenstraw township, Warren county, the name Parsons Wetmore, and Lansing Wetmore, the latter a prothonotary, clerk of the courts, etc., in 1819. Subsequently became a Judge.

WILSON, GEORGE. There are numerous entries in the

name of Wilson in the 1790 Census, for Northumberland county, which, from their close arrangement in the list, were possibly neighbors. Among them we find one George Wilson, single.

TOME LAND WARRANTS FOR LYCOMING CO.

Land Warrants, for Lycoming county, were issued early in the last century to the several Tombs, as follows:
"No. 5, George Tomb, 20 Jany 1815; No. 11, Benjamin Tomb, 12 Feby 1827; No. 12, Samuel Tomb, 17 July 1829; No. 14, George Tomb, 24 Feby 1830; No. 16, Samuel Tomb, 6 April 1830; No. 17, Samuel Tomb, 6 April 1830; No. 18, George Tomb, 5 Augt 1830; No. 21, Benjamin Tomb, 25 April 1831; No. 22, Benjamin Tomb, 11 Novr. 1837;" etc.

ABSTRACTS FROM THE "WARREN MAIL."

DEATH NOTICES.

Frank Tome, son of John and Annette Tome, died 28 April 1854, in Corydon, aged 2 years, 7 months and 12 days.

Sabra Tome, daughter of John and Annette Tome, died 4 May 1854, in Corydon, aged 1 year and 21 days.

Philip Tome, Sr., died 30 April 1855, in Corydon, aged 73 years, 1 month and 8 days.

MARRIAGE NOTICES.

John Tome, of Corydon, and Annette Johnson, of Harmony, Chautauqua Co., N. Y., 21 Sept. 1850, in Corydon.

Benjamin Crooks and Rebecca Ann Tome, both of Corydon, married July 3, 1860, in Corydon.

Masten James and Nancy Tomes, married October 6, 1861, (in Warren).

WILL HIS DREAM COME TRUE?

The Harrisburg *Telegraph*, June 12, 1928, in an editorial, inquires:

"Will the dream of John Tome, of Washingtonboro (Lancaster county), who died a few days since, aged 97, come true? Tome followed the old Pennsylvania canal all his days, until the floods and the railroads combined to close the old waterway to traffic. Then he anchored his boat in the river and waited patiently for the canals to come back. He made the boat his home for many years, and believed to his dying day that one of these times the country would be only too glad to turn again for cheap transportation to the old canals."

BIBLIOGRAPHY

Warren Centennial, 1895.
History of Venango County.
History of Warren County, 1887.
Works of Col. Henry W. Shoemaker.
History of Lycoming County, 1892.
Historical Atlas of Warren County, 1878.
History of Northwestern Pennsylvania, 1905.
Historical Collections of Pennsylvania (Day's).
Colonial Records and Archives of Pennsylvania.
Lycoming County Centennial Association Report, 1896.
Heads of Families, State of Pennsylvania, 1790 Census.
History of McKean, Elk, Cameron and Potter Counties, 1890.

MAPS

Pennsylvania State Highway.
Atlas of Pennsylvania, Bien, 1901.
Historical Map of Pennsylvania, 1875.
Railroad Map of Pennsylvania (Dept. of Internal Affairs).